CW00842799

Soaring In Heavenly Places

Janell Bryant Laughlin

WESTBOW
PRESS®
A DIVISION OF THOMAS NELSON
& ZONDERVAN

Copyright © 2020 Janell Bryant Laughlin.

All rights reserved. No part of this book may be used or reproduced by any means, graphic, electronic, or mechanical, including photocopying, recording, taping or by any information storage retrieval system without the written permission of the author except in the case of brief quotations embodied in critical articles and reviews.

WestBow Press books may be ordered through booksellers or by contacting:

WestBow Press
A Division of Thomas Nelson & Zondervan
1663 Liberty Drive
Bloomington, IN 47403
www.westbowpress.com
1 (866) 928-1240

Because of the dynamic nature of the Internet, any web addresses or links contained in this book may have changed since publication and may no longer be valid. The views expressed in this work are solely those of the author and do not necessarily reflect the views of the publisher, and the publisher hereby disclaims any responsibility for them.

Any people depicted in stock imagery provided by Getty Images are models, and such images are being used for illustrative purposes only. Certain stock imagery © Getty Images.

Scripture taken from the King James Version of the Bible.

Scripture quotations taken from The Holy Bible, New International Version® NIV® Copyright © 1973 1978 1984 2011 by Biblica, Inc. TM. Used by permission. All rights reserved worldwide.

Scripture taken from the Amplified Bible, Copyright © 1954, 1958, 1962, 1964, 1965, 1987 by The Lockman Foundation. Used with permission.

Scripture taken from the New King James Version® Copyright © 1982 by Thomas Nelson. Used by permission. All rights reserved.

ISBN: 978-1-9736-9598-1 (sc)
ISBN: 978-1-9736-9599-8 (e)

Library of Congress Control Number: 2020912135

Print information available on the last page.

WestBow Press rev. date: 07/07/2020

Contents

A Law Written in the Heart

Jeremiah prophesied, "Behold the days come, saith the Lord, that I will make a New Covenant with the house of Israel, and with the house of Judah" (Jeremiah 31:31 KJV). And he prophesied, "After those days, saith the Lord, I will put my law in their inward parts, and write it in their hearts; and will be their God, and they shall be my people" (Jeremiah 31:33 KJV). God has written his law on the tables of our heart (minds). This is the New Law or New Covenant! It is a law that is written on our hearts instead of tables of stone.

Paul said basically the same thing Jeremiah prophesied: "For this is the covenant that I will make with the house of Israel after those days, saith the Lord; I will put my laws into their mind, and write them in their hearts: and I will be to them a God, and they shall be to me a people" (Hebrews 8:10 KJV). He called it *A New Covenant*, and he called the first covenant that God made "Old." He also said, "For that which decayeth and waxeth old is ready to vanish away." It is written in our hearts now so we can live, move and have our being in Christ, following and obeying Jesus. That is the law of liberty – a freedom to obey him. Jesus established a better covenant, through his death, burial, and resurrection, which was much more superior than the old covenant. He *sealed* this new covenant with His blood. It is a law of love, mercy, and grace.

Ezekiel prophesied the same thing: "I will give you a new heart and put a new spirit in you; I will remove from you your heart of stone and give you a heart of flesh" (Ezekiel 36:26 NIV). He also prophesied, "And I will give them *one* heart, and I will put a new spirit within you; and I will take the stony heart out of their flesh, and will give them an heart of flesh; that they may walk in my statutes, and keep mine ordinances, and do them: and they shall be my people, and I will be their God" (Ezekiel 11:19-20 KJV).

We have established by three (3) prophets here a promise from God, that the Lord was going to give us a new heart and put a "new" spirit in us. In 2 Corinthians 13:1 (KJV) Paul said, "In the mouth of two or three witnesses shall every word be established."

God gives it! God puts it in! He is the only one that can change a heart. He is the only one who has the power to renew our mind. He transforms the heart (or mind) by the enlightening power of his living Word. Your change will be one from a hard and unfeeling heart, to a heart that is soft and caring. He will enlarge your territory with himself as your mind is being renewed day by day, from glory to glory. You will become so interwoven with the Lord that you will become as one in him! You will become so closely intertwined that you will take on a nature change. You will become as he is. John said, "As he is, so are we in this world" (1 John 4:17 KJV). The Light of Christ will begin to shine through you.

God wants you to know him. He will give you a heart to know him. Jeremiah also prophesied that the Lord said, "And I will give them an heart to know me, that I am the Lord: that they shall be my people, and I will be their God: for they shall return unto me with their whole heart" (Jeremiah 24:7 KJV).

When the law (of the Spirit) of life in Christ Jesus starts flowing through our veins, we become new creations. We begin losing our appetite for those "old" things of the world. We begin to take on the mind of Christ. We are not what we used to be, just as a butterfly is no longer a caterpillar. A transformation has taken place inside. He turns our dead ashes into something beautiful (life-giving). If any man be in Christ, he is a new creature. No longer are we concerned with earthly things, but with a liberty in the spirit, we begin to soar in heavenly places with peace in our hearts.

This New Covenant would be a *better* covenant, established upon *better* promises. The Apostle Paul wrote, "But now hath he obtained a more excellent ministry, by how much also he is the mediator of a better covenant, which was established upon better promises. For if that first covenant had been faultless, then should no place have been sought for the second" (Hebrews 8:6-7 KJV).

We needed a Savior and Jesus loved us so much that he laid down his own life for us to restore us back into a relationship of love from the heart. Jesus put away the sin-offering. It ended when he offered himself. No more rituals or ceremony. He did not become sin, but he became "the offering" for sin. Jesus had no day by day requirement (as other priests) to offer sacrifices for his own sins (because he knew no sins). He was the Lamb of God, with no spots or blemishes. He *willingly* offered up himself *once* for all. He redeemed us by his blood. He brought total redemption reaching all of his creation - reaching every kindred, every tongue, all people, all nations, every creature in heaven, every creature on the earth, every creature under the earth, in the sea and all that are in them. That sums it up! Total redemption! What a blessing! What a Savior!

Jesus was a sin-offering, but he never sinned. If he had sinned, he would have never qualified to be the Lamb without spot, wrinkle, or blemish. He was the perfect sacrifice, born of a virgin (with God as his Father). He had no sin nature within, so he became the Savior of the world.

There is still hope for us in the new creation man (which is the second Adam or the Lord from heaven – Christ Jesus. Paul said in Hebrews 7:19 (KJV) that "the law made nothing perfect, but the bringing in of a better hope did; by the which we draw nigh to God." The "better hope" is the new creation man – Christ Jesus. In the new man (which is the inner man of the heart), dwells a new nature – the nature of the Father. In his love dwells the law (of the Spirit of life) in Christ Jesus.

God gave Moses the Ten Commandments that was written upon tables of stone. The Ten Commandments were given by God - unchangeable laws that were written by him. With his finger, he engraved them in stone. They were given to bring a restraint to mankind to keep them from destroying themselves. They also showed the weakness of the flesh without God. No matter how mankind tried, he could never live up to the requirements of the law, especially with the 613 additional commandments that were added by Jewish rabbis. If you were guilty of one law, you were guilty of them all. No one could measure up! And, this brought "condemnation" in the lives of the people. They were always feeling guilty about not measuring up!

The stone represented our old hard nature in the first Adam. There can be no life manifested from a law that is written upon stony hearts of the Old Adamic nature. The bible says that the letter kills (because the letter alone does not have any life in it), but the Spirit gives life. There is no "life" in the letter, but when he quickens it with his power, it produces life.

The law that God gave Moses was a law that would be in the heart. "These words, which I command thee this day, shall be in thine heart" (Deuteronomy 6:6 KJV). We can never take the Ten Commandments away for they were given by God, written by his finger.

The old law kept us and preserved us until a birthing of the Holy Spirit. Christ was birthed in our hearts. The old law was a schoolmaster to take us by the hand and lead us to our teacher (Christ). When we became alive in Christ, we no longer needed a schoolmaster, because we have found the teacher who will lead and guide us into all truths.

A heart of stone is a cold heart or a hardened heart. Life can make you that way if you let it. Keep your eyes on Jesus! If you don't, your heart can become hardened with bitterness. This kind of heart is not easily softened. It is an unyielded heart – a heart that prefers walking in darkness rather than light. They detest being around others that walk in Light – those who walk in the Spirit. They are stony hearts, unfeeling, and rebellious. They will even mock those walking in obedience to God. But God can change that stony heart and make it into a heart of flesh. In other words, he can make it new, warm, and caring. He can change your stony heart into a tender heart, a yielded heart, a heart that is always sensitive to the Spirit of God, and quick to repent as David in the bible. He was a man after the Lord's heart. In Acts 13:22 (KJV) the scripture says, "And when he had removed him (Saul), he raised up unto them David to be their king; to whom also he gave testimony, and said, I have found David (the son of Jesse), a man after mine own heart, which shall fulfill all my will."

"Thy word is a *lamp* unto my feet, and a *light* unto my path" (Psalms 119:105 KJV).

In the New Covenant (the law written on our hearts) the Lord speaks. We live, move and have our being *IN* him. As our teacher, he leads and guides us. He has "engraved" His laws upon our hearts and minds. We are no longer under the curse of the Law, for Jesus has set us free from a law (of sin and death). You were set free from the law of sin and death by Jesus Christ.

We are now led by the Spirit of Christ in our inner man. He may speak to us by a gentle tug on our heart, or a still small voice. Christ Jesus said he would teach us his ways; we would walk in his paths.

A New Creation Man

In the Old Testament, the Priest would wash his hands and feet before entering the Holy Place. This is symbolic of cleansing his works and his walk. In the New Covenant, we are now washed by the water of the Word of God. We are a new creation man, created in the image of God in our "inner man of the heart". Old things have passed away and all things have become new.

As the ugly caterpillar is changed into the beautiful butterfly, we are being changed from glory to glory into the completeness of Christ. All the "change" happens inside – from inside out, by the renewing of our minds by the Holy Spirit! It is an *"inward"* spiritual change (or transformation), and you will begin to manifest the nature of Christ "outwardly". You will begin to think straight! When the change begins to take place, others will notice the transformation, for you will no longer be conformed to the ways of the world. "Be not conformed to this world: but be ye transformed by the renewing of your mind, that ye may prove what is that good, and acceptable, and perfect, will of God" (Romans 12:2 KJV).

As our minds are being changed (or transformed) into His image, we become men and women of God that bear the Fruit of the Spirit as mentioned in Galatians 5. Jesus said my Father is glorified if you bear much fruit. Lord make me a fruit bearer.

"Therefore, if anyone is in Christ, he is a new creature: old things have passed away; behold, all things are become new"

(2 Corinthians 5:17 KJV). In Christ, you are a new creation. The change may not take place overnight, but it will happen if you continue to abide in Christ. The ugly caterpillar had to hang onto the limb of the tree (when it was in the dark cocoon), for he knew the season of darkness was going to end, and the change took place in God's appointed time.

When your heart begins to change, the Holy Spirit puts a "new" heart inside of you – a "new" spirit! Your cold stony heart becomes warm and tender. Ezekiel prophesied about the heart being changed. "A new heart also will I give you, and a new spirit will I put within you: and I will take away the stony heart out of your flesh, and I will give you an heart of flesh" (Ezekiel 36:26 KJV).

A Step of Faith

Faith comes by hearing! "Faith comes from hearing the message, and the message is heard through the word about Christ" (Romans 10:17 NIV). Hearing the Word of God increases faith. The ear hears the message of the gospel of Jesus Christ, and the power of the Holy Spirit causes "faith" to arise in the heart. The message may come through an anointed vessel (man or woman) of God when they are preaching. The Holy Spirit will then prick the heart of the unbeliever, drawing him by the Holy Spirit. This is an internal work by the Holy Spirit which causes one to "believe' in Christ. It causes a change to take place in the heart and it is like a "birth" that has taken place inside. You are now persuaded to believe in Christ Jesus, and now have an assurance you never had before – a firm conviction in Christ that nobody can take away. God has given that faith to you. Then you can sing the song, "The world didn't give it to me, and the world can't take it away."

Every man has a measure of faith! Paul said, "Through the grace given unto me, to every man that is among you, not to think of himself more highly than he ought to think; but to think soberly according as God hath dealt to every man the measure of faith" (Romans 12:3 KJV). Faith comes from God. It is not a result of our good works, so we cannot boast about it being a work in our ability, but we know it is a divine work of faith in His ability.

There have been many times in my life when a step of faith was required. Speaking from experience, God has always been faithful. Whenever I felt led by His Spirit to do a particular thing, He was always there to guide me and give me strength to do what he wanted me to do. After taking that one step (a step of faith), God has always been there to assist me on the second step. But we must take that one step!

Sometimes fear may try to overtake you when you are called to do something. Abraham said, "And being fully persuaded that, what he had promised, he was able also to perform" (Romans 4:21 KJV). God has the power to perform (to do) what He has promised. When I was singing in church, ministering before the people, or waiting at the airport to get on a plane, I have always depended on this promise from God, "I can do all things through Christ who strengthens me" (Philippians 4:13 KJV). When fear would try to hinder me, I would remember in the scripture that "God is not a man that can lie." I actually believe that God wants us to put him to the test, so he can prove himself to us. When my legs trembled from fear when I got up to minister or sing before the people, his power always caused me to triumph. He always came through for me and proved himself. That was plenty of "evidence" to me that He is Lord. That was plenty of "proof" that He is God.

"Now faith is the substance of things hoped for, the evidence of things not seen" (Hebrews 11:1 KJV). Faith is having the "confidence" in the promises of God, a "believing" in what He said. Our natural (visible) eyes may not see it yet, but we know that faith will see the *invisible* things (by the Holy Spirit). Faith is the "assurance" that they will be seen. It is a knowing that we will see the "evidence" or "proof" of things not yet seen.

In Malachi 3:10 (AMP) it says, "to prove Me now by it, says the Lord of hosts, if I will not open the windows of heaven for you and pour you out a blessing, that there shall not be room enough to receive it," God will reward you by your obedience. If you feel a particular thing to do on your heart, then go ahead and take that *one step of faith* and God will give you His strength to do what He has called you to do. I can speak from experience that after taking that first step of faith, all fear left. His power was greater than my fears. His strength was made perfect in my weakness!

Walking by faith is "putting the Word of God into action." When you take one step by faith, God will take the second step with you. The apostle Paul told us that "faith without works is dead". If God is leading you to do something on your heart, take that first step (of faith) as Abraham did, when God spoke to him to leave his country, taking nothing with him. All the men of faith in the Old Covenant acted on their faith.

I want to mention three women of faith in the bible: There was a woman of Canaan, a gentile woman, a woman who must have been very troubled for her daughter, and she had such a mother's love that she took a step of faith for her. In much distress, she came and cried unto Jesus, saying, "Have mercy on me, O Lord, thou son of David; my daughter is grievously vexed with a devil." The disciples said, "Send her away!" She persisted and came to Jesus and worshiped him, saying, "Lord help me!" Jesus answered and said, "It is not right to take the children's bread, and toss it to the dogs" (Matthew 15:26 NIV). She was a gentile, which at that time was considered to be no more than dogs to the nation of Israel at that time. But she spoke in faith and said, "Truth, Lord; yet the dogs eat of the crumbs which fall from their masters table." I believe she was saying that if the dogs can eat the crumbs, certainly you can give me a crumb, just one crumb of healing for my daughter. Then Jesus answered, and said unto her, "O woman, great is thy faith: be it unto thee even as thou wilt." And her daughter was made whole from that very hour.

Rahab was another woman from Canaan, a gentile, who lived in the city of Jericho. She was known as a harlot. She hid the two Israelites who had come to spy out the land in Jericho, before the Israelites captured the city. The bible said, "By faith, the harlot Rahab perished not with them (that believed not), when she had received the spies with peace" (Hebrews 11:31 KJV). Her faith plus her actions pleased God. "For as the body without the spirit is dead, so faith without works is dead also" (James 2:26 KJV). We can have faith, but we need to take a step of faith to do what God us to do. God gives us a desire, then He gives us the ability to carry out what He wants us to do. By faith, Rahab took a step of faith and made a way for the two Israelites to escape. Because of her faith, her family was saved, and the whole family.

There was a certain woman that had an issue of blood for 12 years. She had suffered so long until she probably was about to give up on any thought of healing for herself. She had been to many physicians and none could help her. She spent all that she had, and every day grew worse. She had "heard" of Jesus, and I'm sure her faith was increased after "hearing" about Jesus. She was probably weak in her condition, and desperate to do something. She had a "got to do something" kind of faith. So, when Jesus came by, she came behind him, and touched the hem of his garment. For she said within herself, "If I may but touch his garment, I shall be made whole" (Matthew 9:21 KJV). She did not have a doubt at all, but instead a firm assurance He would heal her. Jesus said to her, "Daughter, be of good comfort; thy faith hath made thee whole" (Matthew: 9:22 KJV). The woman was made whole that very hour.

If God is calling you to do something, and you feel a release in your spirit, go ahead and take the first step of faith. You can depend on God, for he will be there to help you take the second step.

Can The Tongue Be Tamed

Although James said, "No man can tame the tongue," he did not leave us without hope. For he told us there is something we can do, "Resist the devil and he will flee from you." Then he told us how to resist the devil - by "yielding!" It is the opposite of what our flesh is wanting to do. If we let our minds go wild, we will speak anything that comes to mind. We need to yield and humble ourselves in the sight of the Lord. "Submit yourselves therefore to God." (James 4:7 KJV). By submitting ourselves to God, we are yielding to Him, like a soldier volunteering to obey his commanding officer. We are to be in subjection to Christ Jesus at all times. We can close the door to the enemy - not even cracking the door for an opportunity for the enemy to work. To submit to God is giving in to Him. It is surrendering and letting Him do what we cannot do. He is the one who can tame the tongue. That's where the power comes from - the power of the Holy Ghost!

Chickens And Eagles

Chickens wait to be fed (by others), but eagles feed themselves!

Many are living in a barnyard capacity, but there are those "called" (by God's grace) to live in a higher order of the Spirit!

On our big farm in South, Georgia, I heard about a farmer that was raising baby chickens, and someone gave him a baby eagle. Day by day as he fed the chickens and the eagle, he began noticing little differences between them. As they began to grow, he noticed the chickens were always "looking down," pecking in the dirt on the ground. They represent a people who are content where they are, just living comfortably as they bear the image of the "earthly." On the contrary, eagles do not fit in with the chickens! They are never satisfied living on the ground for they feel a higher calling inside. Eagles are born with a desire to fly in the heavenly places! If God has called you to a higher walk, you are like that eagle, for an eagle instinctively knows that he is not born for the barnyard (a lower form of existence). As the eagle begins to grow, he feels a stirring (or longing) for the higher place. He begins to "look up," and as the wind begins to blow, he lifts his wings and begins to soar up higher – in heavenly places. The wind represents the Spirit! It carried him into a higher place without him having to flap his wings or struggle. He just raised his wings, and the Lord did the rest. The wind carried him "in" it, just as we are carried "in Christ." From glory to glory the Lord is bringing about a change inside of us. He gives us his strength and power to rise above any circumstance, as we have our minds firmly "fixed" on the prize of the high calling of God "in" Christ Jesus.

Count It All Joy

"Consider it pure joy, my brothers and sisters, whenever you face trials of many kinds, because you know that the testing of your faith produces perseverance" (James 1:2-3 NIV). James goes on to say that the "trying" of your faith works patience. Then he said to "let patience finish its work so that you may be mature and complete, not lacking anything." Perseverance means "not giving up" even when it is hard, but to hang in there until God has accomplished what He has started in you. Can we count it all joy?

There is no oil without the "pressing" of the olives; no wine without the "pressing" of the grapes; no beautiful fragrance without the "crushing" of the rose petals; no joy without sorrow.

Eagles Must Rest

It's of a necessity that sometimes the big eagles have to descend from the high heavenly places in the sky to take a break and rest. When he becomes tired and weary, he realizes that he will need a set of fresh feathers – a lot of strength to fly back into the heavenlies. God must refresh him once again with vitality and strength because he will need it again and again.

The eagle knows by instinct that he must rest sometimes. He knows he can't survive on his own strength, but this strength must come from within him. Then after taking time to rest, he is once again refreshed and ready to go again. So it is in our lives. Sometimes we need to realize that when we become tired and weary, we must realize that our strength comes from the River of Life that flows from within. We must come aside and draw strength from our heavenly Father.

At the appointed time, the wind will blow again, and all the eagle has to do is just lift his wings (not flapping or working), and the wind (which represents the Spirit) causes him to rise up again. He rises by the power of the wind (Spirit).

We, too, will be refreshed when we set ourselves aside and come unto Jesus. We will arise and be refreshed to do what we need to do, by the power of the living God that lives inside of us. We as eagle saints must realize that we cannot endure by our own strength but by the strength of the Lord. We can do all things through Christ who gives us strength. Take time to rest and draw strength from the power of God. To set ourselves aside at times and staying quiet before the Lord is not wasted time, for during this time, God is filling us with his power and might. By His power, He always causes us to be lifted up again. The same power that caused Jesus to be raised from the dead dwells in us. Without this energizing power of God, we cannot endure.

Entanglements

The apostle Paul wrote a letter to Timothy (his son in the faith) encouraging him to endure hard times as a good soldier of Jesus Christ. He wrote, "No man that warreth entangleth himself with the affairs of this life; so that he may please him who hath chosen him to be a soldier" (2 Timothy 2:4 KJV). We will always be engaged in some kind of warfare in this life, but we are not to get so involved with matters that it hinders our "calling" by God. And only you and the Lord know what that particular calling is. My calling has been in music, but I didn't neglect my responsibilities. I supported my husband (a preacher) and raising two children. All of us worked as a team for years. Several years later after our children were older, I began to have a desire to do some writing. I began to post little writings on Facebook. One day I received a message from a lady in India, and she said the writings were really blessing her. She asked if she could publish my writings there. She was a Christian and teacher. That's when I got more involved in writing, knowing it was blessing many people. That's how my writing began - the Lord leading all the way. I began to hear from others in India and how they were uplifted and encouraged. Later, my husband went on a trip there and met Esther Queeny Tantati, and he was there for a dedication of my booklets. The booklets were given out to many pastors during a conference. See how the Lord works. He gives us a desire, then the ability to carry out that desire. Later the Lord led me into publishing my first paperback book called, "Soaring Upward," in the United States of America. My first book was done at age 71, and the Lord is renewing my strength day by day. I am working on my 2nd book now at the great age of 75. The book is called, "Soaring In Heavenly Places." He promised he would restore our youth like the eagles!

The Lord led me into writing, and I have learned so much from studying the word of God. It brings me great peace to find hidden treasures in the word as I study. But many things have tried to hinder me and my time writing the book. People began to call and wanting me to begin singing with them. One church wanted me to become a worship leader. I did get involved with the church but didn't have peace in my heart. I had to quit doing that and get back to the passion the Lord laid on my heart. I had become "entangled" into doing something that others wanted me to do. Doing the music was not wrong within itself, but one needs to do what God puts on their heart. The Lord said, if we love him, we will keep His commandments.

As a river flows freely, we must be free like that. The Lord has blessed me abundantly, not with a lot of money but a peace in my heart. It has not always been easy, but the Lord helped me to endure every day. We must give ourselves wholly to whatever the calling is to please the Lord, and it is He that has called you. You didn't call yourself. He called you to do whatever the task may be. He has chosen you for that particular purpose. You won't be happy trying to fill somebody else's shoes.

The world is like an octopus with many arms pulling us into many directions. We are to be free of all entanglements, and not become ensnared (caught in a trap), like a fly caught in a spider's cobweb. In the army of the Lord, we must keep our focus on how we can please the Lord. As a soldier thinks how he can please his commanding officer, we too must hearken unto the voice of the Lord, and please him – and not let the world sap the "life" out of us. I've seen fish after they have been caught in a net, and I've seen a bear caught in a bear-trap. That's what can happen to us. We will be caught in a trap (entangled in the affairs of this world), and it will choke the life out of you. If we don't let the world reel us in (as the fish that is reeled in), we will have a freedom and peace inside, a peace that passes all understanding.

To be free of entanglements will liberate us to live, move and have our being in Christ Jesus. The apostle Paul said, "Stand fast therefore in the liberty wherewith Christ hath made us free, and be not entangled again with the yoke of bondage" (Galatians 5:1 KJV). As a prisoner is released from captivity, so happy are they when they are loosed. If any of us are held captive to anything or anybody, we are as a slave. Jesus said, "It is written: Worship the Lord your God and serve him only" (Luke 4:8 NIV).

"For if after they have escaped the pollutions of the world through the knowledge of the Lord and Saviour Jesus Christ, they are again entangled therein, and overcome, the latter end is worse with them than the beginning" (2 Peter 2:20 KJV). If the air has too much exhaust fumes from vehicles, the air becomes polluted, and is not clean or pure. If our water becomes polluted, we will install a water filter in the faucet to purify the water. So it is in the spirit! If our minds are polluted or preoccupied with the affairs of this world, it can hinder you from having peace in your heart. Things become much clearer if we keep ourselves from being "contaminated" by the affairs of this world.

Jesus talked about those, which when they have heard, go forth, and are "choked" with cares and riches and pleasures of this life, and bringing no fruit to perfection – Luke 8:14 KJV.

Paul said, "Wherefore come out from among them, and be ye separate, saith the Lord, and touch not the unclean thing; and I will receive you" (2 Cors.6:17 KJV). A soldier as long as he is enlisted in the military, devotes himself to the service of his country. That's his main purpose – to separate himself from all other matters and serve his country. We should be just as devoted to Christ. God has chosen you to be a good soldier in the army of the Lord.

Fruit of The Spirit

The Apostle Paul talked about the nine (9) "fruit" of the Spirit in Galations 5:22-23 (KJV): The scripture calls it "fruit," NOT "fruits." There is only ONE fruit of the Spirit and that is the Spirit of Christ that is produced in us from Him. Paul said that the "fruit" of the Spirit is love. Then he goes on to list the other characteristics (or manifestations) of His love - I prefer to call these "manifestations" of His love, for when one manifests something, it is an outward visible expression for the world to see. When we are bearing the fruit of the Spirit, we are manifesting Christ in the earth. The only Christ that people will see is when you are manifesting Him to the world. The apostle Paul is listing the nine fruit of the Spirit as: love, joy, peace, longsuffering, gentleness, goodness, faith, meekness, temperance. Galatians 5:22-23 (KJV).

All the manifestations of the Fruit of the Spirit (according to Paul) *bud* out of the Love of Christ. This is an "agape" love, an unconditional love, a love which expects nothing in return. It is a willing love coming from the heart. A great example of this great love was when Jesus went to the cross "willingly" and died for our sins.

A spiritual "gift" is freely given to us, but the "fruit" of the Spirit has to be produced in us so that we can give. When we are bearing fruit, we become the givers.

To bear or produce this "fruit" of the Spirit, we must submit to the Holy Spirit of God, and let Him do his work in us. Sometimes a lot of pruning must take place for us to bear fruit.

In John 15:1-2 (KJV) Jesus said, "I am the true vine, and my Father is the husbandman. Every branch in me that beareth not fruit he taketh away, and every branch that beareth fruit, he purgeth it, that it may bring forth more fruit."

The Vine is filled with all the life that comes up out of the Root (Jesus), but the branches (us) are the ones bearing the Fruit of the Spirit. I am part of the Vine and He is now a part of me. The branches bear what He is – Fruit of the Spirit. We are braided together as One.

"Have the roots [of your being] firmly and deeply planted [in Him, fixed and founded in Him], being continually built up in Him" (Colossians 2:7 AMP). Out roots will go down deep if we continually abide in the Vine (Christ), praying, meditating and studying the Word of God. We will be like a tree planted by the rivers of living water. We will be firmly fixed in Him (Christ). You will grow up or be "built up" in Him. Then when the storms come and they will, your root will be so strong, you will not waver and be tossed to and fro like waves on the ocean, for Jesus is our Root.

The Apostle Paul said, "That he would grant you, according to the riches of his glory, to be strengthened with might by his Spirit in the "inner" man; that Christ may dwell in your hearts by faith: that you being rooted and grounded in love, may be able to comprehend with ALL SAINTS what is the breadth, and length, and depth, and height; And to know the <u>love of</u>

<u>Christ</u>, which passeth knowledge, that you might be filled with all the fullness of God" (Ephesians 3:16-19 KJV).

We can receive a "gift" of the Spirit, but not be walking in love (not bearing fruit)!

The spiritual "gifts" are freely given, but the "fruit" of the Spirit has to be produced in and through us before we can bear this kind of love-fruit.

Gifts of The Spirit

The Apostle Paul lists *nine* (9) spiritual "gifts" of the Spirit. All nine of these gifts operate by that same Spirit, and God distributes to every man, as HE wills. A "gift" of the Spirit is freely given. You didn't have to work for it. You didn't have to earn it. It's from the Lord to benefit the body of Christ. There are listed nine gifts – but it is the same Spirit who gives them, and it is given freely from the Lord (as He wills). Here are listed nine gifts of that one (self-same) Spirit: "To one is given by the Spirit the <u>word of wisdom</u>; to another is given the <u>word of knowledge</u> by the same Spirit; to another <u>faith</u> by the same Spirit; to another the <u>gifts of healing</u> by the same Spirit; to another the <u>working of miracles</u>; to another <u>prophecy</u>; to another <u>discerning of spirits</u>; to another <u>divers kinds of tongues:</u> to another the <u>interpretation of tongues,</u> but all of these worketh that one and the selfsame Spirit, dividing to every man severally as He will" (1 Corinthians 12:8-11 KJV).

God distributes (divides) gifts individually to every man as He wills (by His grace). Men have different gifts, but it is the same Spirit who gives them. It is beneficial for the body of Christ when He gives a gift to the Believer, but Paul talks about the "more excellent" way – the way of love. He gives gifts to those He chooses, so we cannot boast within ourselves about having a particular gift, for it is a gift freely given by God by His grace. We didn't earn it! It was freely given!

The Lord gives gifts to those as He wills, and when He gives a spiritual "gift," it does not mean they are bearing "fruit" of the Spirit. The sweet "Fruit of the Spirit" or the "nature" of the Lord has to be produced inside of you by the Holy Spirit.

Before the nature of The Lamb (Jesus) is produced in us, a change or transformation by the Holy Spirit is necessary. You begin to grow spiritually, and it is a process from being a babe in Christ into a full-grown mature man.

Paul said that the *"more excellent way"* was to bear fruit. These are his words: "But covet earnestly the best gifts: and yet show I unto you a more excellent way" (1 Corinthians 12:31 KJV). Paul was saying that a "gift" is beneficial for the body of Christ, but the "more excellent way" is to bear the Fruit of the Holy Spirit. All manifestations of the Spirit must at the same time manifest the ways of love. Without love, all manifestations of a "gift" is as a clanging cymbal – it just makes a show and a lot of noise.

Paul said, "Though I speak with the tongues of men and of angels, and have not charity, I have become as sounding brass, or a tinkling cymbal. And though I have the gift of prophecy, and understand all mysteries, and all knowledge; and though I have all faith, so that I could remove mountains, and have not charity, I am nothing. And though I bestow all my goods to feed *the poor,* and though I give my body to be burned, and have not charity, it profiteth me nothing.

Charity suffereth long, *and* is kind; charity envieth not; charity vaunteth not itself, is not puffed up; doth not behave itself unseemingly, seeketh not her own, is not easily provoked, thinketh no evil; rejoiceth not in iniquity, but rejoiceth in the truth; beareth all things, believeth all things, hopeth all things, endureth all things.

Charity never faileth. But whether *there be* prophecies, they shall fail; whether *there be* tongues, they shall cease; whether *there be* knowledge, it shall vanish away. For we know in part and we prophesy in part. But when that which is perfect is come, then that which is in part shall be done away" (1 Corinthians 13:1-10 KJV). Love never fails! In other words, without love it is just a lot of noise – a lot of showmanship!

A spiritual "gift" is *freely given* to us, but the "fruit" of the Spirit has to be *produced* in us so that we can give. When we are bearing fruit (or walking in love), we become the givers.

All spiritual "gifts" are given by God to the body of Christ, but they are nothing without love (charity), for His love never fails.

God Is Like A Refiner's Fire

" The fining pot is for silver and the furnace for gold, but the Lord trieth the heart" (Proverbs 17:3 KJV). God wants hearts that are refined - a people pure (in heart).

God is like a refiner's fire. He is separating the truth from the false - the wheat from the chaff! Our God is a "consuming fire" working within, creating a pure heart. He is like a blazing hot fire that refines metals, or like a strong soap that bleaches clothes removing all spots and stains, making us clean and white (pure). A heart with no spots or stains! He is doing a work within each of us, and it's a process. "But who may abide the day of his coming? and who shall stand when he appeareth? for he is like a refiner's fire, and like fullers' soap: And he shall sit as a refiner and purifier of silver: and he shall purify the sons of Levi, and purge them as gold and silver, that they may offer unto the LORD an offering in righteousness" (Malachi 3:2-3 KJV).

There is a process of refining silver. The Silversmith holds the piece of silver over the hot fire. He holds it in the middle of the fire where it is the hottest. As it melts, the dross rises to the surface and he skims it off. Then the process continues again. He holds it in the hot fire and as it melts, the dross/impurities rise to the surface, and he skims it off. Over and over the process continues until the process is completed. When it is completed (or refined), the silver shines, and the Silversmith can see his likeness or image in the silver. During the process of the hot fire being applied, there is a separation that takes place. The Precious Metals (gold and silver) melt, but do not burn like the other materials. The heating of the gold or silver only destroys the dross, leaving the "pure" alloy.

There is a process of separating the chaff from the wheat. A farmer only removes the chaff (husks of corn) that has been separated from the wheat by a threshing. Through this process, he leaves the wheat unharmed. On our journey in life, we may have many trials, and sometimes it feels like we are even put into the hot oven, but it is through this fire of being baked (processed), that God removes the impurities. The wheat is then used to make into bread to feed others.

God doesn't want to destroy us. He is removing anything unlike Himself for He is a God of love. In this process, we are being conformed into His image. In this process, He is like a Fuller's soap, washing us clean and creating a "pure" heart within us. This very strong soap (like potash), will even remove all stains and spots.

Our God is a consuming fire. The Lord told Jeremiah to go down to the potter's house and consider the work taking place on the potter's wheel. After the clay is fashioned into whatever the potter wants, he then puts it into the hot oven. The heat will show any defects in the pottery. If the pottery is defective, with tender compassion, he breaks it and starts the process all over again.

1 Peter 4:12-13 (KJV) it says, "Beloved, think it not strange concerning the fiery trial which is to try you, as though some

strange thing happened unto you: But rejoice, inasmuch as ye are partakers of Christ's sufferings; that, when his glory shall be revealed, ye may be glad also with exceeding joy." Our faith is being tested by the fiery trial which comes our way. Did you take notice of the word "trial?" One trial! A constant, daily, moment by moment trial, and constantly being changed from glory to glory. It is a spiritual growing process. Peter said that the "trial" of your faith is precious. Your faith is much more precious than the perishable gold which is tested and purified by fire.

There was a King Nebuchadnezzar who had made an image of gold (90 ft. high and 9 ft. wide). He had the image set up on the plain of Dura in the province of Babylon. On the day of dedication, he ordered everyone to fall and down and worship the image of gold – his god. His orders were for anyone who did not worship this image (or god), to be thrown into a fiery furnace. There were three Jews that he had set over the province of Babylon who refused to bow down to this image of gold that King Nebuchadnezzar had set up. The king was in a rage because of this and ordered the furnace to be heated seven times hotter than usual. He ordered some soldiers to tie the three up and throw them into the fiery furnace. The flame from the furnace was so hot that it killed the soldiers. The furnace had to be at least 1,000 degrees Fahrenheit. The King was so surprised, because as he stood on his feet, he said, "Lo, (or look), I see four men loose, walking in the midst of the fire, and they have no hurt; and the form of the fourth is like the Son of God" (Daniel 3:25 KJV). For the heat to be turned up seven times, is a lot of purifying, but in the middle of our fiery trials, there is always one with you, and he said he'd never leave or forsake you. His name is Jesus! Remember, it is God refining you! David said, "The words of the Lord are pure words; as silver tried in a furnace of earth, purified seven times" (Psalms 12:6 KJV). As He refines us, we become more and more like him, our Creator. He is creating in us a clean heart and renewing a "right" spirit.

We are tried by the fire of the Holy Ghost. It is not to destroy us but to change the sin nature inside of us. A scripture from Jeremiah 23:29 (KJV) says, "Is not my word like as a fire? saith the Lord; and like a hammer that breaketh the rock in pieces?" Everyone at one time or another goes through something that, if left to themselves, could destroy themselves. God has a purpose and a plan for everyone, and nobody escapes him.

"After you have suffered a little while, the God of all grace [who imparts all blessing and favor], who has called you to His [own] eternal glory in Christ Jesus, will Himself complete, and make you what you ought to be, establish and ground you securely, and strengthen, and settle you" (1 Peter 5:10 AMP).

Something that has been "refined" has gone through a process to remove impurities – like an oil refinery that removes impurities from the oil.

For musicians, they cringe when an instrument has not been tuned properly. But when it is "in tune" it is so pleasant to hear. That's what it feels like to be around one refined.

When a person is not refined, it shows in his character. He may talk too loud, too much, or too fast not considering the feelings of the other person. He may not be tactful, have bad manners, vulgar, curse, and not treat people with respect. But it is so pleasant to be with a person that is "refined." You can bet that this person has gone through the fire. They are usually good listeners, slow to criticize, and are very tactful in their speech. They do not speak in a harsh tone, and do not belch at the table when eating. They are quick to lift a person up when they feel low.

You can tell right away if a person has been "pruned." Refined and pruned! A lot of pruning takes place in our lives to be refined (bearing fruit). To bear or produce this "fruit" of the Spirit, we need to submit to the Spirit of God, and let Him do his work in us. Jesus said that every branch that does not bear fruit He takes away, and every branch that bears fruit, he purges it, that it may bring forth more fruit.

David said, "For you, O God, have proved us; You have tried us as silver is tried, refined and purified" (Psalms 66:10 AMP).

God Loves A Cheerful Giver

To be a cheerful giver, one must always give from the heart. "Every man according as he purposes in his heart, so let him give; not grudgingly, or of necessity; for God loves a cheerful giver" (2 Corinthians 9:7 KJV). The act of giving should be an offering of the heart. As the Lord lays it on your heart, give. But do not give out of obligation or necessity just because you feel forced or pressured. But if you give according to the purpose in your heart, you will give freely which brings a happiness from within. It is a joy unspeakable and full of glory. We are not to give grudgingly, meaning "not of grief," for if you do, you will be grieved in your spirit, making you feel sorry that you gave.

The apostle Paul pointed out to us that we must remember the weak. And, we must remember the words of Jesus when he said, "It is more blessed to give than to receive" (Acts 20:35 KJV). What a joy it is just to be able to give, and to give generously as God speaks to your heart. Do not hold back when God speaks to your heart to give. If you have a desire to be generous, cast your bread on the waters, for you are going to get it back, for it will come back to you. "Cast your bread upon the waters, for you will find it after many days" (Ecclesiastes 11:1 AMP). You won't have to worry, for if God tells you to give and you obey, he will return it to you. He does not always return it to you with money. It could be a new job or a raise on your job. It could be in your health.

It says in 2 Corinthians 9:6 (KJV), "But this I say, he who soweth sparingly shall reap also sparingly; and he which soweth bountifully shall reap also bountifully.

There is much need in the body of Christ for a more "giving" and "forgiving" spirit. Instead of harboring ill feelings toward your brother or sister, *let us give more forgiveness.* Peter came to Jesus and asked him how often his brother sin against him and he forgive. He asked if seven times would be enough. Jesus said to him, "I tell you, not up to seven times, but seventy times seven" (Matthew 18:22 AMP). That is a lot of forgiveness, an unlimited amount of forgiveness – an unlimited measure. The word "forgiveness" means to let go; to set free; or to release. An example would be to release a little bird out of a cage. When you release (or free) the little bird, he is filled with joy to have a freedom he never had before. He begins to be happy and sings unto the Lord. And, after you have released it to the Lord, you are freeing yourself. You are the one freed!

"Give, and it will be given to you. A good measure, pressed down, shaken together and running over, will be poured into your lap. For with the measure you use, it will be measured to you" (Luke 6:38 NIV). When something (such as a bowl of flour) is pressed and shaken, it will spill over into your lap, for the bowl can hold no more. God will pour blessings into your lap. God has promised you that if you give, He will return it to you.

God can return it to you by "natural" blessings or by "spiritual" blessings.

A great sign of spiritual maturity is when one gives freely and walks in obedience by the law which is written on his heart – the promptings of the Holy Spirit.

To be joyful, one must be a giver. If we sow kindness, we will reap kindness. Give a smile and watch how people react. Cook a good dinner for your husband. Help someone struggling pay a bill. Sometimes worship leaders get discouraged at church because a lot of people just stare, not helping with the singing. I can identify with this one! If you begin to sing along, she will get encouraged. Telephone someone (instead of text messaging) and hear their voice perk up. I love to hear my son and daughter's voice. It makes my day! Spend precious time with your children, for you will reap a great reward when they grow up, for they are copying you. You are their example! Speak a positive word into your children. Tell them that "They can do all things through Christ who strengthens them." I heard a story of an elderly lady who had lost her husband and had very little food. One day someone begin walking up to her door out of concern. She told him she did not know who was bringing the food, but the Lord was providing. She was getting a full return for the many years of "giving."

The amount of "giving" you give, that same amount will be measured unto you.

A farmer who plants only a few seeds will only get a small crop. But the one who plants generously will get a generous crop. And if the farmer generously plants an abundance of seeds, God will reward him with a harvest, providing more than enough than he needs – with plenty left over.

A great example of a willing and cheerful giver was Jesus Christ. He was as one seed in the earth. When He died, His life was released for all mankind, that all who believe, might freely partake of him and all might live by Him. This one seed remained as only one single seed until he died. But when He died, it produced many seeds. He gave up his life on the cross, *willingly* for us, so that his very "life" could be released into the earth. His return would be a kingdom of many glorious sons. The bible says, "Except a corn (kernel) of wheat fall into the ground and die, it abideth alone, but if it dies, it bringeth forth much fruit" (John 12:24 KJV).

Every man according as he purposes *in his heart*, so let him give, for God loves a cheerful giver.

Guidelines For Giving

The guideline for giving to God and His work is found in 2 Corinthians 9:6-7 (KJV), "But this I say, he which sows sparingly shall also reap sparingly; and he which soweth bountifully shall also reap bountifully. Every man according as he purposed in his heart so let him give; not grudgingly, or of necessity; for God loves a cheerful giver." What a joy when one gives as God lays it on his heart. We are not to give grudgingly, meaning "not of grief," for you will be grieved in your spirit, and you will feel sorry you gave - it grieves you. It can cause feelings of resentment and bitterness. That is what Jesus ended - a law to make us do something out of necessity, but from the heart, a free heart. I actually give more this way! Don't you like giving from your heart? There is a freedom in it! But let not this freedom become a stumbling block to you. Give, give, give and then give some more. This is a great sign of spiritual maturity when one does not have to be coerced, pressured, forced, threatened, bullied, made to give.

Heaven's Design of Blue

G od made no secret of His great design
And what He created was right on time
He draped the sky with the color "blue"
In my eyes it was such a heavenly hue

The great Creator was very wise
To create a color just for our eyes
He made no mistakes and knew what to do
He filled the sky with a curtain of "blue"

The color "blue" so pure and light
Tells me everything is going to be alright
Descending low and toward my face
Coming from such a high and lofty place

A curtain of "blue" so impressively high
Shows such a noble place as it fills the sky
God's favorite color for others to view
The sky was filled with the color of "blue"

Hidden Manna

G od told Moses to take some of the Manna that had fallen from the heavens and place it in the Ark of the Covenant. Jesus told us some very powerful words in the Book of Revelation 2:7 (KJV), "To him that overcomes will I give to eat of the tree of life, which is in the midst of the paradise of God." A great promise! To him that overcomes will he give to eat of the hidden manna. You may ask what is this hidden manna? It is the bread from heaven.

Jesus told us, "I am the living bread which came down from heaven: if any man eat of this bread, he shall live forever: and the bread that I give is my flesh, which I will give for the life of the world" (John 6:51 KJV). The Jews therefore strove among themselves saying, "How can this man give us his flesh to eat?" Then Jesus said unto them, "Verily, verily, I say unto you, Except you eat the flesh (Word) of the Son of Man, and drink his blood (Spirit), you have no life in you" (John 6:53 KJV).

John tells us, "The Word was made flesh, and dwelt among us, (and we beheld his glory, the glory as of the only begotten of the Father,) full of grace and truth" (John 1:14 KJV).

You are now the ark of God. He is living inside of you. No longer in the box (Ark of the Covenant). You are the tabernacle of God. God lives inside of you if you know his son Jesus Christ. God is revealing himself to his people. A God of love, mercy, compassion, and tenderness - much different than most of us were taught while growing up. Solomon says so beautifully, "I am my beloved's, and HE is mine." As the chorus says we used to sing, "His Banner Over Me is Love!" We are eating from the hidden manna. *The manna is the revelation of Jesus Christ.* Spiritual food from the heavens! Even as we need "natural" food for the natural man to grow, we need "spiritual" food for the inner man of the heart to grow.

O taste and see that the Lord is good as the psalmist tells us.

Hidden Treasures

In the Christ which lives inside of you are all the treasures of wisdom and knowledge. He is no longer far away. He now resides in us. What a glorious revelation that we have the creator of the universe living inside of us. We are the temple of God. We are the house HE lives in now. We are now the living ark that carries the glory of God. Most of Christianity is not aware of this. They pray to a God that lives on the other side of the milky way. Of course, he does live there as well, but I want to emphasize a point that we are the Holy Temple that is not made by hands now. No hammer or nail was used to build this temple for we are the temple that God is building. We are his workmanship. His presence covers all that he has created. What a mighty God we serve. And yet in all of his glory, he still has the heart of a father towards his children. His love is measureless. Jesus told us, "I am come that you might have life, and have it more abundantly." The meaning of *"more abundantly"* means measureless. It is that well inside of you that Jesus spoke of; it is the spiritual rivers of living water that would flow out of your innermost being, as Jesus said in the book of John.

The scripture says, "That their hearts might be comforted, being knit together in love, and unto all riches of the full assurance of understanding, to the acknowledgement of the mystery of God, and of the Father, and of Christ; In whom are hid all the treasures of wisdom and knowledge" (Colossians 2:2-3 KJV). Even the mystery which has been hid from the ages and generations, but now is made manifest to his saints: To whom God would make known what is the riches of the glory of this mystery among the Gentiles: which is Christ in you, the hope of glory" (Colossians 1:26-27 KJV).

The prophet (Ezekiel) spoke some powerful words, "And I will scatter thee among the heathen, and disperse thee in the countries, and will consume thy filthiness out of thee. *And thou shall take thine inheritance in thyself in the sight of the heathen, and thou shalt know that I am the Lord" (Ezekiel 22:15-16 KJV).*

In 2 Corinthians 4:7 (KJV) Paul again tells us some powerful words, "But we have this treasure in earthen vessels, that the excellency of the power may be of God and not of us." Isn't it wonderful that we can eat of the hidden manna which is the Christ (treasure) hidden in our earthen vessels.

Hope To The End

O ne night after going to bed, I felt a little troubled in my spirit because so many in this day are losing hope. Many are giving up! Lying on my bed I began to pray, for I was feeling a little weary myself. After falling asleep, I began to have a dream about "hope." In the dream, I heard myself speak these words out loud, *"Hope to the end."* I looked in the Strong's concordance to find the meaning of these words. In 1 Peter 1:13 (KJV) it says, "Wherefore gird up the loins of your mind, be sober, and hope to the end for the grace that is to be brought unto you at the revelation of Jesus Christ." We must be sober-minded (spiritually alert) and be aware of how the enemy can bring hopelessness into our lives. "Be sober, be vigilant; because your adversary the devil, as a roaring lion, walketh about, seeking whom he may devour" (1 Peter 5:8 KJV).

"Hope deferred maketh the heart sick, but when the desire cometh, it is a tree of life" (Proverbs 13:12 KJV). When hope is deferred (withheld, put off, or delayed), we can become heartsick in the waiting process. In the process of the waiting period there can be many hindrances that can occur before we see our desires fulfilled but hang on. Your day is coming! There will be an end to your despair! Like a child in the mother's womb for nine months, the mother can become very weary carrying the baby around for nine months in her body. But when the child is born and the mother sees the beautiful child breathing with life, her desire has been fulfilled. God hears every tear you cry, and He knows every little heartache. I have personally seen some of my desires fulfilled after praying about some matters for many years. I stood before a congregation one time and told them no matter how bleak this particular situation seemed, they would hear me say one day, "Look what the Lord has done!" And God worked a miracle. The miracle happened several years later but it happened. Do not allow the enemy to cause you to quit. Submit to God and he will give you the desires of your heart. Many times on our journey, we may have many disappointments that leave us feeling heartsick, but this will eventually pass just as a storm that comes and goes.

The apostle Paul referred to "hope," as an anchor of the soul. He said, "Which hope we have as an anchor of the soul, both sure and stedfast, and which entereth into that within the veil" (Hebrews 6:19 KJV). On a ship, an anchor keeps the vessel from drifting away, due to the current or wind. It keeps the ship in a certain position, holding it in place. Well, that's what Christ Jesus is to us. He keeps us steady when we feel as if we are drifting away. In Christ Jesus is a hope that will keep you steady, steadfast and immovable when the world is trying to pull you away from abiding in Him. In 1 Corinthians 15:58 (KJV) it says, "Therefore my beloved brethren, be ye stedfast, unmoveable, always abounding in the work of the Lord, forasmuch as ye know that your labour is not in vain in the Lord." To have this kind of hope, one must always abound in the work of the Lord, and you can have the assurance that your labor (in the Lord) is not in vain. This labor is not necessarily doing what man always wants, but doing what the Lord wants you to do. If you get caught up in always doing what man wants you to do, your labor will be in vain, and it will cause you to get too weary and exhausted, and cause you to lose your hope in Christ.

Did you know that the mystery of God is "Christ in you, the hope of glory!" The apostle Paul said, "Even the mystery which hath been hid from ages and from generations, but now is made manifest to his saints: To whom God would make known what is the riches of the glory of this mystery among the gentiles; which is Christ in you, the hope of glory" (Colossians 1:26-27 KJV). He was saying this mystery (secret things) of Christ in the saints of God was going to be made manifest – made known. It would be Christ dwelling inside of you, living inside of you, walking and talking with you. Christ in you, the "hope" of glory. Christ is our hope, our Rock (refuge).

There is hope to the end! The outcome of a matter will be greater. Set your eyes on the prize, the goal. Do not give up and quit. Get alone with the Lord in the secret place of the Most High, and pray. Meditate on His word. David said, "I wait for the Lord, my soul doth wait, and in His word do I hope." God's promises are true, and He never fails.

Joel prophesied, "The Lord will be the hope of his people, and the strength of the children of Israel" (Joel 3:16 KJV). The Lord is our hope and he is our strength.

My anchor holds and grips the solid Rock (Jesus). Look unto Christ for He is your hope.

"There is *hope in thine end*, saith the Lord, that thy children shall come again to their own border" (Jeremiah 31:17 KJV). Just as the prodigal son came home to his father, you too, can come home anytime, for His mercy endures forever.

I Am Redeemed

A missionary told some people in slavery about being redeemed so they could better understand it. The missionary said, *"God took your necks out - out of the iron collars you are wearing. God redeemed you! You are no longer slaves (unable to free yourselves) from any sin. I am here to tell you that Jesus Christ has freed you - redeemed you by His own precious blood. He has taken your neck out of the collar."* The precious blood of the Lamb (Jesus) did that for us. He has taken our necks out of the iron collar. No longer are we slaves to anyone or anything.

We love the Lord so much that we have become as bond-slaves to him. We are free, yet we choose to remain with him and serve him - our Lord and Savior (Jesus Christ). If you put a little bird in your hand and he wants to fly away, and you hold onto him so tightly that he can't fly, at the first opportunity he gets, he will probably fly away and never come back home; but if you loose him and let him fly away freely, he will fly away, but will eventually come back home because he will remember that this dwelling place was where he found unconditional love and acceptance. In the world you will not find this kind of love and acceptance. But you will find it in the secret place of the Most High. On the cross Jesus set us free. He loosed us and restored us back to a place of freedom in the Spirit to live, move and have our being in him. The Father always rejoices when one of his children comes back home. You can always go back home. Aren't you glad that you have been redeemed! He freed us from being a slave to sin. Jesus paid the price. He bought us with his own blood. He loosed us. A return to the same place/ glory we had in God before the world began. I am re-deemed!

We have been redeemed because of the precious blood of the Lamb. That Lamb is Jesus Christ! "You were not redeemed with corruptible things, as silver and gold, from your vain conversation received by tradition from your fathers; but with the precious blood of Christ, as of a lamb without blemish and without spot, who verily was foreordained before the foundation of the world, but was manifest in these last times for you" (1 Peter 1:18-20 KJV). He was foreordained in the flesh for our redemption, but he had to be made manifest. A Savior (without sin) had to come for our redemption. We needed a Savior! One without blemish, no spot or even a wrinkle, but a perfect sinless lamb.

Jesus <u>willingly</u> went to the cross and gave his life, and his blood atoned for all sin.

Jesus' blood was called "precious" meaning it was very valuable and costly. The blood of the Lamb was costly because it was the life of God. This is the precious blood that washes away all our sins. We were in bondage to a power within us, slaves to our own beast nature because of the fall, but Jesus gave his life/blood so we would not have to live that way. The "life" is in the blood. When he gave his life, his blood, he poured out his blood-life so we could once again have a right relationship with our heavenly Father. He brought us back to God as his own purchased possession.

Something precious was paid for you, but it was not with silver or gold (corruptible things), but with the precious blood of Jesus. Your body now belongs to the Lord. "Know you not that your body is the temple of the Holy Ghost which is in you, which you have of God, and you are not your own? For you are bought with a price: therefore glorify God in your body, and in your spirit, which are God's" (1 Corinthians 6:19-20 KJV). Your body is God's! Your spirit is God's. You belong to Christ. If you are bought, then you are not your own. You are the Lord's property, so we need to take care of our body which is the temple of God.

You are bought with a price, by the blood of Jesus. The blood of Jesus was so great that the value could not be estimated. It was priceless!

"Neither by the blood of goats and calves, but by his own blood he entered into ONCE into the holy place, having obtained eternal redemption for us" (Hebrews 9:12 KJV).

This Lamb of God was Jesus, a sacrificial Lamb, a Lamb without spot, wrinkle or blemish. A sacrificial and sinless Lamb of God who could bring us out of spiritual slavery (out of darkness of sin) into His light. "But ye are a chosen generation, a royal priesthood, an holy nation, a peculiar people; that ye should shew forth the praises of him who hath called you out of darkness into his marvellous light" (1 Peter 2:9 KJV).

Christ Jesus rescued you from sin and death by his blood. His blood fixed the gulf that separated us from God. We were made nigh by the blood of the Lamb. "I have blotted out, as a thick cloud, thy transgressions, and, as a cloud, thy sins: return unto me; for I have redeemed thee" (Isaiah 44:22 KJV).

"Who gave himself a ransom for all, to be testified in due time" (1 Timothy 2:6 KJV). Jesus gave *himself* as a ransom for all. He became our ransom by giving his own life. He gave himself as a ransom-price to free us from bondage. Jesus did that. He paid the price for us with his life-blood. He freed us! No longer are we held captive in sin.

"In whom we have redemption through his blood, the forgiveness of sins..." (Ephesians 1:7 KJV). We have been redeemed, and we now have boldness to enter into his presence at this very hour. Through his blood we have forgiveness of sins. We can come boldly now before him and confess our sins and he so willingly wipes them away. He loves us because he is our Father.

I have been redeemed, bought and paid for in full, by the precious blood of Jesus. He is our Redeemer! He turned us loose, and set us free so we would not have to live as a slave anymore, but live as a free son, to come and go as we please. And we aim to please our heavenly Father. He wants us to be free to live, move and have our being in Him for He is a Father who loves us!

John Pointed to Christ

John the Baptist was ordained to be the "herald" of Christ! He announced the coming of the Lord Jesus Christ!

"John did *no* miracle, but all things that John spoke of this man (Jesus) were true" (John 10:41 KJV). John was sent by God to bear witness of the Light. John was not that Light (but was sent to bear witness of that Light) that all men through him might believe. He was not sent to be "seen," but to be a "voice" of one crying aloud in the wilderness saying, *"Make straight the way of the Lord."*

John did no miracles, yet what an honor and a privilege when John announced the coming of the Lord, beholding (by the Spirit) that Jesus was the Son of God. Then he spoke these words: "Behold the Lamb of God which taketh away the sin of the world."

John was filled with the Holy Ghost, even from his mother's womb. [Luke 1:15] He was sent to point men to Christ, so his main purpose was to make ready the hearts of the people for the coming Messiah - Jesus. He would tell them that he was not the Christ, but that he was sent before Christ.

John said, "He (Jesus) must *increase*, but I (John) must *decrease*" (John 3:30 KJV).

There were no miracles performed by John, yet Jesus said, "Verily I say unto you, among them are born of women, there hath not risen a greater than John the Baptist: notwithstanding he that is least in the kingdom of heaven is greater than he" (Matthew 11:11 KJV).

John prepared the Way for the greatest miracle of all – *salvation* which was brought by our Lord and Savior, Jesus Christ!

Little Foxes

It's the "little" foxes that spoil the vine! The "little" foxes are trying to sneak into my vineyard, and they are very sly and cunning. They come in without making a lot of noise, as quiet as can be, but we know they are there. Foxes are very crafty, and subtle. They chew and bite on the little branches and leaves, and dig holes, leaving the roots exposed, which destroys the plant. We must beware of the "little" foxes!

The Lord (my beloved) is removing from us all of those "little" foxes" that spoil the vines. "Take us the foxes, the little foxes, that spoil the vines: for our vines have tender grapes" (Solomon's Song 2:15 KJV). We pray you take us (or from us) those "little" foxes that want to destroy the vine in our lives, which keeps us from producing fruit. As David prayed, "Create in me a clean heart, O God; and renew a right spirit within me" (Psalms 51:10 KJV).

"My beloved is mine, and I am his" (Solomon's Song 2:16 KJV). We are as a bride following her Lover into His chamber to have an intimate love relationship, to be made one with Him. But there are so many "little" foxes that are trying to sneak in to destroy our most intimate love.

Before the tender grapes appear, we must break away and hearken to the voice of the Lord and come away with Him (our Beloved). "For, lo, the winter is past, the rain is over and gone; the flowers appear on the earth; the time of the singing (of birds) is come, and the voice of the turtledove is heard in our land; the fig tree puts forth and ripens her green figs, and the vines are in blossom; they give forth their fragrance. Arise, my love, my fair one, and come away. [So I went with him, and when we were climbing the rocky steps up the hillside, my beloved shepherd said to me] O my dove [while you are there], in the seclusion of the clefts in the solid rock, and in the sheltered and secret place of the cliff, let me hear your voice, for your voice is sweet, and your face is lovely. [My heart was touched and I fervently sang to him my desire] Take us the foxes, the little foxes, that spoil the vineyards [of our love], for our vineyards are in blossom" (Solomon's Song 2:11-15 AMP).

Father, my Beloved, "Take (from us) the foxes, the little foxes, that spoil the vineyards (of our love), for our vineyards are in blossom." Catch the little foxes! These "little" foxes are trying to come in to destroy my vine to keep me from walking in the Kingdom of God. It's those "little" subtle things that are trying to hinder me from dwelling in the secret place of the Most High. The cold harsh winter season is over. The rain is over, and the sun is shining brightly. I see beautiful blossoms giving forth a wonderful fragrance. The birds are singing! A New Season is here – Spring is here! It is a New Day – New Beginnings! Lord, you are so lovely. Every day spent with you gets sweeter and sweeter as the day goes by!

I believe a "big" fox is the power of the tongue. "The tongue is a little member, and boasteth great things. Behold how great a matter a little fire kindleth" (James 3:5 KJV). As a child, I used to go into the woods to gather fatwood (kindling) whenever I wanted to start a fire. I would start the fire, then put kindling on it, and it would become a bigger fire. The same thing can happen if we are gossiping, slandering, and backbiting. It is like a fire that gets out of control and can devastate lives, ruining reputations, even though the person may have repented of past sins.

A little leaven leaveneth the whole lump. When yeast/leaven is added into the dough, it causes the whole mass of dough to rise (or get bigger). The dough has to be put into a very hot oven for the bread to be made. The hot fire in the oven causes a transformation to take place inside the dough, and when the fresh bread is made, it is so good. Many times the Lord brings a chastening in our lives to show us our weaknesses, because He wants us to come to him and have a special intimate love relationship with us (in the Spirit), because he loves us so much – just like you desire your children to come into your arms to love you. It usually takes the fire of the Holy Ghost to burn the little foxes out. If you endure chastening (by yielding to the Lord), God deals with you as a son. If you are rebellious, God will remove that "little" fox in His time and in His way!

The bible warns of false prophets in the land that are foolish, that follow their own spirit, and have seen nothing – Ezekiel 13:3 AMP. That is a characteristic of a fox, walking in craftiness, using good words that people want to hear, deceiving the hearts of many.

To produce healthy grapes, the vines must be pruned every year. With proper pruning, the grapevines will be more manageable and have better fruit. Without pruning, the vines grow wild, and not produce any fruit. The trimming can make a difference between a good crop and a bad one. We want tender sweet grapes, and without the pruning in our lives, we would never come to maturity. We would be like a baby on a pacifier, never growing up. Jesus is the Vine and we are the branches. For the branches to produce fruit, it is necessary for the branches to go through a pruning (or a cutting away). John said, "Every branch in me that beareth not fruit he taketh away: and every branch that beareth fruit, he purgeth it, that it may bring forth more fruit" (John 15:2 KJV). Come Lord, take us (or from us) the little foxes that spoil or ruin the vine. Help us to yield to your Spirit, so we can produce your sweet nature in the earth. Make us as your tender grapes, sweet to the taste.

Men of Faith

"By *faith* he (Moses) forsook Egypt, not fearing the wrath of the king; for he endured, as seeing him who is invisible" (Hebrews 11:27 KJV). Moses was a man who walked by faith. He endured (steadfast in faith) as seeing him who is invisible. We know he could not see God with his natural eyes, for God is a Spirit. He took God at his word and believed that whatever God told him that it would come to pass. The only way we can walk by faith is by remaining steadfast, trusting the Lord enough to take the first step, and to walk in obedience. God had a purpose for Moses' life, and it was 80 years before he would be in the position to deliver Israel. He had a walk of faith, in what God had promised, he was able to perform (to do). According to the Jewish historian (Josephus), Moses was next in line to be Pharaoh of Egypt. When he became of age, he refused to be called the son of Pharaoh's daughter, choosing rather to suffer affliction with the people of God than to enjoy the pleasures of sin, esteeming the reproach of Christ greater riches than the treasures of Egypt. He turned his back on all of the glories and riches of Egypt to find a better way. He learned the better way on the back side of the desert. He was a man who was in line for the throne of Egypt! He was a man who had lived a life of pleasure! The man who spoke orders to men and they obeyed without anyone questioning him! At one time, he had to tend his father-in-law's sheep. He did not even have any sheep of his own. The man who had led thousands in Egypt was humbled, and now leading sheep. Think of the humiliation, for God stripped him of his glory. He worked humility into him, for the scripture said, "Now the man Moses was very meek, above all the men which were upon the face of the earth" (Numbers 12:3 KJV). God had finished a great work in Moses. He was now the meekest man on the face of the earth, had finally found the purpose God wanted for his life, and went on to fulfill what God had called him to do. A great man of faith!

Another man of faith was David. He was called to be the king of Israel and found himself hiding from Saul in fear for his life. One time he was in despair because his own son Absalom was trying to kill him. In the book of Psalms, it talked about him as a great man of faith. He fought the giant Goliath and defeated him. When discouragement would try to overtake him, he would always encourage himself in the Lord. Even though he had a rag tag army of the outcasts of society, he defeated his enemies. He never looked back. When faced with impossibilities he would encourage himself in the Lord and win the battles. He walked by faith and not by sight.

Joseph was a man of faith - the little boy who found "favor" by his father. This almost cost him his life. His brothers were very jealous of him. He was thrown into a pit and sold into slavery. He found himself thrown into the dungeon because of false accusations made against him. That does not sound like someone who has a great call of God on their life does it? Joseph later told his brothers, "But as for you, you thought evil against me, but God meant it unto good, to bring to pass, as it is this day, to save much people alive" (Genesis 50:20 KJV). So, when your faith is being "tried," just be patient and wait on the Lord, for He will turn it around for your good.

Joshua and Caleb were the only two of the original twelve spies that were allowed to enter the promised land. All of the older generation perished in the wilderness. These two men walked by faith and believed the word of the Lord. Caleb had faith when he told the people to be quiet before Moses, and said, "Let us go up at once, and possess the land." They did not look at circumstances, but were strong in faith giving glory to God believing that what he had promised he was able to perform (to do). The scripture said that the sun and the moon stood still a whole day for Joshua when he prayed to God, in order for them to have time to complete a victory. A man of great faith.

God spoke to Martin Luther the scripture, "The just shall live by faith!" This changed Martin Luther, and eventually the world, by his obedience. He helped bring in the Protestant Reformation and changed the church world.

A Roman centurion came to Jesus and asked him to heal his servant who was sick of the palsy and grievously tormented. The centurion felt unworthy that Jesus came under his roof, but said to him, "speak the word only, and my servant shall be healed" (Matthew 8:8 KJV). He told Jesus that he was used to giving orders and seeing them obeyed and carried out, and Jesus marveled and said to him, "Verily, I say unto you, I have not found so great faith, no not in Israel" (Matthew 8:10 KJV). The servant was healed as soon as Jesus spoke the word.

There was a woman of Canaan who came and cried unto Jesus, saying, "Have mercy on me, O Lord, thou son of David; my daughter is grievously vexed with a devil" (Matthew 15:22 KJV). The disciples said, "Send her away!" She came to Jesus and worshiped him, saying, "Lord help me." Jesus answered and said, "It is not meet to take the children's bread, and to cast it to dogs" (Matthew 15:26 KJV). He said this to her because the Gentiles were considered no more than dogs to the nation of Israel at that time. Then the woman spoke in faith and said, "Truth, Lord: yet the dogs eat of the crumbs which fall from their masters' table." Then Jesus answered, and said unto her, "O woman, great is thy faith: be it unto thee even as thou wilt." And her daughter was made whole from that very hour.

Mount Up on Eagles' Wings

"They that wait upon the Lord shall renew their strength; they shall mount up with wings as eagles; they shall run, and not be weary; and they shall walk, and not faint" (Isaiah 40:31 KJV). Arise eagle saints!

Did you know that eagles get very excited when a storm is approaching? They know that when a storm comes, it will bring lots of wind. He loves the wind, for the greater the wind, the higher he soars. The eagle uses the wind to his advantage, and spreading his wings, he soars upward - off the low places with ease. No struggle is needed at this time, and he just remains in a "fixed" position awaiting the right time to simply spread his wings, letting the wind do the work. In the bible, the wind represents the Holy Spirit. If you have a problem, or if you get a bad diagnosis from your doctor, do not fear, for the power of our living God will arise with healing in His wings, and cause you to soar in heavenly places, and cause you to arise, even in the midst of all of your adversities. He will lift you up into higher heights of the Spirit. Jesus will arise in your heart, and comfort you. If you remain in a "fixed" position and wait on the Lord, He shall renew your strength, and you shall mount up with wings as an eagle. You shall run, and not be weary; you shall walk, and not faint. That is why the bible refers to us as "eagle" saints.

The very sight of an eagle *lifts* my spirit. When you behold an eagle soaring in the high distant blue sky, with freedom and grace, you know why eagles are "king of the birds." They portray a beautiful picture of grace. Even when descending to the earth below, they show discipline in catching their prey. They are aware of the fact that they hold higher altitudes than other birds in the sky, exhibiting majesty in flight with their eight-feet wing span, with a swiftness in the open (free) air! I love the fact that they portray an authority and confidence in the high places, and seem to really enjoy the freedom in the air with such keen eye vision. Their vision is six to eight times better than ours, and can spot an object as small as a rabbit from a distance of two miles.

The secret to an eagle's strength is his waiting! They that "wait" upon the Lord shall renew their strength. He instinctively knows he must wait. He knows there is a secret in having patience - "waiting" for the right time to act. And at the right time, he plunges downward, catching his prey with his powerful talons. He has an assurance that all is well. He knows that he is "master of the air."

In Isaiah 30:15 (AMP) it says, "...*in quietness and in [trusting] confidence shall be your strength.*"

The eagle in flight seems to convey a message that none of the other birds convey - free of all constraints. They can even soar directly toward the sun and not be harmed. And while soaring directly toward the sun (with two eyelids protecting their eyes), their enemies cannot pursue them. It is from the sun they get their bearings and find their way home after long forays in search of food.

Eagles do not waste energy on doing all the "works" of flying like the other birds, struggling or flapping their wings, but know they are called to a higher place, and can use the wind currents (that have already been provided freely) to lift them higher and higher. Although gravity keeps trying to "pull him down," they always break loose from its stronghold. The gravity is counteracted, and he is pushed upward. This upward thrust comes from a rising current of air. Then an even more powerful up-current comes when the sun heats the ground, causing the warm air to rise. In the ascending columns of this warm air, the eagle soars with *no effort* and is carried upward higher and higher. It is breathtaking to see them in a circle going round and round on these warm air currents soaring effortlessly. They just *rest* on these thermal warm updrafts.

The eagle has an instinctive trust to do what he must do. He simply trusts in God, free from worry, soaring where others fear to trod. He is like a "finger pointing toward the ways of God." We can observe them in the open air as if they are saying to us, "Discover the enormous lifting power of faith!"

After the death of King David and King Solomon, Israel began to rapidly decline, but right in the middle of the decline, God sends comfort to his people. He sends a word by the prophet (Isaiah) with these comforting words from Isaiah 40:31, *"They that wait upon the Lord shall renew their strength; they shall mount up with wings as eagles; they shall run, and not be weary; and they shall walk, and not faint."*

Eagles are capable of reaching higher altitudes than any other birds. They have been seen soaring almost motionlessly in near hurricane-force winds, trusting the power of the wind to take him where he needs to go.

Eagles have powerful talons for gripping their prey. They are not comfortable on the ground, unlike a vulture which is content to walk on the ground. They love to soar in heavenly places, and have been seen in hurricane force winds!

Resting time! There is always a need for resting time. Sometimes the eagle gets very tired and exhausted. He knows that in order to dwell in the high places, he has to do something contrary to what the world teaches - *"waiting on the Lord,"* for he knows that he needs an abundance of energy to soar in the heavenlies. He recognizes his need for some "quiet" time. He needs an environment of quiet isolation, a time of "waiting before the Lord. He knows this time of *waiting is not wasted time,* but is needed for him to be energized once again with strength and power. So at this time, he separates himself from the world, to this hidden place, where there is water that is fresh and clear. He has realized that a change must come. While being in that hidden place, drinking of this fresh water, he does not work. He does not hunt because his beak and talons have become dull. He loses his feathers!

He retreats to this hidden place (in the Spirit), then begins to drink of "fresh water."

A transformation begins to take place. His feathers begin to grow back out. His beak becomes like new second teeth. His powerful talons grow back and are sharp once again. He then sharpens his beak on the rocks (representing Jesus, our Rock) to make it razor sharp (the Word of the Lord is sharper than any two-edged sword).

Underneath the eagles' wings are pockets of oil which he breaks. He begins to shine and glisten in the sunlight. He knows the healing power of the sun's rays as he lies "eagle spread" on a ledge in the sun (represents the healing power of the Son).

Now the eagle is now refreshed again! He has an unconquerable spirit coming from within. He is ready to soar again. No longer tired and weary! He knows it is time to soar once again into the heavenlies. With a "new" determination, he "mounts up" and locks his wings in place, then uses the wind to his advantage launching himself onto the currents of the wind. It is joy unspeakable!

We are eagle saints! We can soar into the heavenlies of the Spirit. We can use the wind of the Holy Spirit to our advantage. At times we become tired and weary, and in those times, we are in dire need for some quiet time. Time to just bask in His presence, connecting our spirit to His. Then the healing power of the Son (Jesus) will bring a refreshing in us, and we will become energized with His strength. "...I bare you on eagles' wings and brought you unto Myself" from Exodus 19:4 KJV.

An eagle is the opposite of a snake, for he is not comfortable on the ground. A snake is a creeping creature living on the ground, abiding in low places. He is deadly, wise and powerful, yet when an eagle spots him, he can sweep down and can carry him off into the air where he is defenseless. In the air, the snake has no power – there in the high places. Stay in the high places – the high places of the Holy Spirit. Abide there and the enemy we face will be powerless and defenseless. He is defeated by Christ Jesus, for Jesus has stripped him of his power and gave us authority over all our enemies. Mount up with wings as an eagle.

Natural Vs. Spiritual

There is a *natural* body, and there is a *spiritual* body (1 Corinthians 15:44 KJV). The apostle Paul made comparisons of the two. He compared the natural body to the spiritual body so we could better understand how the "spiritual" body of Christ functions! The spiritual church is not the building where you go, because the building is natural. There is nothing spiritual about it because it is dead, having no life inside. The only life is in the Spirit of God! The Spiritual church is the TRUE church - the body of Christ, with Christ as the Head. He said that you first have a natural body (with a head), with many members (toes, fingers, feet, arms, etc.), and the body cannot do without the head, and the head cannot do without the body. It is the same in the Spirit. The spiritual body, the True Church, is the body of Christ (with many born again believers/members). The Head of this spiritual true church is Christ Jesus our Lord. The wonderful thing is that he loves us so much that He wants and needs a place to lay His Head - in his body - the body of Christ. That is us - the spiritual living church. We cannot live without the Head, and the Head (Jesus) cannot function without us. We need each other. We (the body of Christ) need Christ (the Head) to guide us always. We cannot separate the body from the Head. As the natural body is dead without the Head, so the spiritual body is dead without the Head (Jesus). It will not function right and will not produce any Life!

Nothing by Any Means

Nothing shall "by any means" harm you." Nothing "by any means" or any stretch of the imagination shall harm you! Nothing shall "in any way possible" harm you! Jesus said, "Behold, I give you power to tread on serpents and scorpions, and over <u>all</u> the power of the enemy, and nothing shall by any means hurt you" (Luke 10:19 KJV). This comforting scripture came to my mind one day as I began to worry about my loved ones during a Coronavirus Pandemic in the United States in 2020. The Lord brought this scripture back to my remembrance! That is why we need to hide the Word of God in our hearts, because when we need comforting, he will comfort us! Jesus said, "The Comforter, which is the Holy Ghost, whom the Father shall send in my name, he shall teach you all things, and bring all things to your remembrance, whatsoever I have said unto you" (John 14:26 KJV). So today, the Lord was comforting me with these words that nothing "by any means" or nothing "at all" would harm me.

The Lord said that HE would give you power! He would give you the authority to tread on (or upon) anything that would cause you to fear. "Who shall separate us from the love of Christ? Shall tribulation, or distress, or famine, or nakedness, or peril, or sword?" (Romans 8:35) KJV. The apostle Paul said that we are more than conquerors through him that loved us, and nothing shall "by any means" separate us from the love of God, which is in Christ Jesus our Lord.

Reconciled to God

When a man and woman fall in love, the love they have for each other becomes so strong that they have a desire to become united as "one." A marriage takes place between the two. So much harmony exists between the two. They walk hand in hand with each other. The relationship is wonderful, and their attention is always focused on each other. They have eyes like a dove. A dove does not have peripheral vision, but always looks straight ahead, focusing their whole attention on the one they love. The two (as one) love each other with all their hearts, but somewhere along the line, they failed to guard their hearts. The close relationship that they had is eventually affected, and they drift apart from each other in their hearts. The once loving relationship has become distant, and sometimes even to the point of hostility. They may become enemies in their hearts. They become like strangers in their own home. They may become estranged (strange) yet live in the same house. The marriage ends!

Spiritually speaking, the relationship between man and God ended because of sin - because of the first Adam. He failed to guard his heart with Eve. Sin entered the camp! Man's heart was against God. He was self-centered, filled with his own ways – a heart filled with enmity against God. Because of sin, man was estranged, and alienated from God. The close relationship between man and God that was once experienced in the garden of Eden as they walked hand in hand ended.

God's mercy endures forever! God had a plan! That plan was to bring back the harmony between man and Himself. He loved us so much that He wanted to patch things up and reconcile man back unto Himself. He wanted to restore us so we could have a fellowship with him once again. That is what the word "reconcile" means! It's a restoration of friendly relations between two parties who are estranged! *A synonym would be: kiss and make up; declare a truce; bury the hatchet. That is exactly what Jesus did! He settled the account!*

Thanks to our Lord and Savior (Jesus Christ), we have now been reconciled to God by the shedding of his blood on the Cross. The relationship between man and God has been restored. The apostle Paul said, "And all things are of God, who hath reconciled us to himself by Jesus Christ, and hath given to us the ministry of reconciliation" (2 Corinthians 5:18 KJV). The believer is created anew (in the heart), and the change came by the mighty power of God, for only God can change a heart. He made the heart new again. "Therefore, if any man be in Christ, he is a new creature: old things have passed away; behold, all things are become new" (2 Corinthians 5:17 KJV).

What a gift from God with his great plan of reconciliation, to reconcile us to Himself. Our relationship has now been *restored*. Our relationship has now been restored into a wonderful state of harmony. Musicians know a lot about harmony! When a person is off key singing, it is not a good sound, but now we hear the wonderful sound of harmony between ourselves and God in our hearts, and it is such a peaceful sound. We are now made nigh by the blood of Christ, and we are now friends. "For if, when we were enemies, we were reconciled to God by the death of his Son, much more, being reconciled, we shall be saved by his life" (Romans 5:10 KJV). By his death we are reconciled, and by his life we are saved.

God loved us so much that he wanted to *restore* the relationship brought on by the fall of man. His great plan was to send his only son Jesus (the Redeemer of the whole world) to re-establish friendly relations once again with mankind – to restore that harmony again.

Jesus reconciled us unto Himself on the Cross, and now we have received the message in our hearts, the ministry of reconciliation, "to witness that God was in Christ, reconciling the world unto himself, not imputing their trespasses unto them; and hath committed unto us the word of reconciliation" (2 Corinthians 5:19 KJV). Paul was telling them (us) that "we" have a message, a ministry to preach the gospel of peace to the whole world.

Paul said in Colossians 1:20-22 (KJV), "And, having made peace through the blood of his cross, by him to reconcile all things unto himself, by him, I say, whether they be things in earth, or things in heaven. And you, that were sometime alienated and enemies in your mind by wicked works, yet now hath he reconciled. In the body of his flesh through death, to present you holy and unblameable and unreproveable in his sight." God had a plan. A plan to reconcile to Himself everything on earth and everything in heaven. We were once strangers (strange) to God, and spiritual enemies. But now he welcomes us into his presence. We can walk hand in hand with Jesus! We have been redeemed, restored, reconciled by the blood of the Lamb!

We are being changed from glory to glory. We must fill our minds with His Word. We must guard our hearts and not let hindrances pull us into the world to distract us from our "first" love. If we abide in Christ, then He abides in us! We are walking hand-in-hand! A marriage is taking place within us as our desire toward him is wonderful and peaceful. Our nature is being changed into the image of Christ, just as an ugly caterpillar is changed into a beautiful butterfly. And the more we are changed from inside, the more peace in our hearts and minds we will have.

If you have hard feelings against your brother, kiss and make up; bury the hatchet; declare a truce.

Soaring Eagles

D id you know that eagles get very excited when a storm is approaching? They know that when a storm comes, it will bring lots of wind. He loves the wind, for the greater the wind, the higher he soars. The eagle uses the wind to his advantage, and spreading his wings, he soars upward - off the low places with ease. No struggle is needed at this time, but he just remains in a "fixed" position awaiting the right time to simply spread his wings, letting the wind do the work. In the bible, the wind represents the Holy Spirit. If you have a problem, or if you get a bad diagnosis from your doctor, do not fear, for the power of our living God will cause you to soar in heavenly places, and cause you to arise even while in the midst of all of your adversities. He will lift you up into higher heights of the Spirit. Jesus will arise in your heart, and comfort you. If you remain in a "fixed" position and wait on the Lord, He shall renew your strength, and you shall mount up with wings as an eagle. You shall run, and not be weary; you shall walk, and not faint. That must be why the bible refers to us as "eagle" saints.

Sought Out

You shall be called, "Sought Out." People will begin to seek you out just to hear a word from the Lord, a word of wisdom. They will see how blessed you are. They will say, "Look what the Lord has done" in you. You will have a word of wisdom to give them. "They shall call them, *The holy people, The Redeemed of the Lord*; and thou shalt be called, *Sought Out, A city not forsaken*" (Isaiah 62:12 KJV).

The Queen of Sheba had heard about Solomon's great wisdom, and she travelled far to meet him! After she met him, heard his wisdom, and saw the great house with its many riches in it, she was in awe. She did not believe what she had heard until she saw it with her own eyes. She said, "the half was not told me: thy wisdom and prosperity exceeded the fame which I heard" (1 Kings 10:7 KJV).

Many will seek to find you, for you will have wisdom to be all things to all people. The apostle Paul speaking in humility said, "To the weak became I as weak, that I might gain the weak: I have become all things to all men, that I might by all means save some" (1 Corinthians 9:22 KJV). Paul never wanted to offend the weak, for he wanted to win them over to Christianity. He even said, "But take heed lest by any means this liberty of yours become a stumblingblock to them that are weak" (1 Corinthians 8:9 KJV). If meat offended his brother, he would not eat it if it caused him to be offended. The same way in dress, customs and manners. With a clear conscience, he wanted to win them over. Paul stated that he "endured all things for the elects' sakes, that they may also obtain the salvation which is in Christ Jesus with eternal glory" (2 Timothy 2:10 KJV).

The Chinese Bamboo Plant

The Chinese Bamboo Plant is a wonderful example of our Christian walk. The seed of the plant lies dormant in the earth for four (4) years. The plant has to be nurtured and cared for during this time period. During this time period, the root of the plant is being established, growing down deep, and becoming strong. No matter what is happening outside, the plant is preparing itself to enter the world strong. The apostle Paul said in Ephesians 3:16-18 (KJV), "That he would grant you, according to the riches of his glory, to be strengthened with might by his Spirit in the "inner" man; that Christ may dwell in your hearts by faith: that you, being rooted and grounded in love, may be able to comprehend with all saints what is the breadth, and length, and depth, and height; And to know the love of Christ, which passeth knowledge, that you might be filled with all the fulness of God."

After God has placed his seed (Word-Christ) in our hearts, there is a process we go through. Just as a baby is born, he drinks milk and cannot eat solid food. But little by little, as he begins to grow, he begins to eat strong meat. By spending time with our Lord, he is teaching us how to be strong. And it is only through Him that we become strong. Through fellowship with the Lord we become as the apostle Paul exhorts us in Ephesian 6:10 (KJV), "Finally, my brethren, be strong in the Lord, and in the power of His might."

After the four-year period, the Chinese Bamboo Plant has developed a strong root system. The root goes down deep so it will be able to support the tall plant when it begins to break through the soil. On the outside it appears that nothing has taken place, and looks as if the seed will never grow, but it will.

"Have the roots [of your being] firmly and deeply planted [in Him, fixed and founded in Him], being continually built up in Him, becoming increasingly more confirmed and established in the faith, just as you were taught, and abounding and overflowing in it with thanksgiving" (Colossians 2:7 AMP). Out roots will go down deep if we continually abide in the Vine (Christ), praying, meditating, and studying the Word of God. We will be like a tree planted by the rivers of living water. We will be firmly fixed in Him (Christ). You will grow up or be "built up" in Him. Then when the storms come and they will, your root will be strong, and you will not waver and be tossed to and fro like waves on the ocean. *Jesus is our Root.*

On the fifth year, it looks like a miracle! A change begins to take place within the Chinese Bamboo plant! Within a short six-week period, it can grow 80 feet tall. And you do not have to worry about the plant for it has a great root system. Remember, the Root is Christ Jesus!

The number five (5) symbolizes God's grace - his goodness and mercy, for his mercy endures forever. In John 1:16 (KJV) it says, "And of His fulness have we all received, and grace for grace." The number five is mentioned 318 times in the Scripture. That's a lot of grace.

In the Word of God we have many examples of the farmer planting a seed and then having long patience for the seed to come up and produce after its kind. The seed of corn will produce corn. The seed of melons will produce melons and so on. The seed of God (Word) will produce the fruit of the Spirit: *love, joy, peace, longsuffering, gentleness, goodness, faith, meekness, temperance.* Galatians 5:22-23 (KJV).

Jesus said these powerful words in John 15:8 KJV, "Herein is my Father glorified, that you bear much fruit; so shall you be my disciples." God is looking for men and women who will be fruit-bearers.

The only way to be a fruit-bearer is to know him (Jesus). Paul said in Philippians 3:10 KJV, "That I may know him, and the power of his resurrection, and the fellowship of his sufferings, being made conformable unto his death; by any means I might attain unto the resurrection of the dead."

As we look around us sometimes, it seems as if nothing is happening. On the outside there seems to be little change, but on the inside a marvelous transformation is taking place. We are being transformed into the image of Christ. And just as the Chinese Bamboo plant took on an a visible form (an outward expression), we are being changed from glory to glory so much that the "hidden man of the heart" which is Christ, begins to show Himself to the world (an outward expression or manifestation of Christ). Christ shows Himself to the world by showing what He is – kindness, gentleness, and all the "fruit of the Spirit." In 2 Corinthians 3:18 (KJV) it says, "But we all, with open face beholding as in a glass the glory of the Lord, are changed into the same image from glory to glory, even as by the Spirit of the Lord."

"But let it be the hidden man of the heart, in that which is not corruptible, even the ornament of a meek and quiet spirit, which is in the sight of God of great price" (1 Peter 3:4 KJV). The "hidden man of the heart" is the Spirit of Christ. An inner beautiful essence becoming an outward expression in the earth.

The same thing that happened to the Bamboo Plant is happening inside of us. It's a progressive (inward) work taking place inside of us. Our root goes down deep and wraps itself around the Rock which is Christ. When the storms of life come (and they will), we will be prepared to lean upon the Lord for strength and guidance.

As a wise man named King Solomon once said in Proverbs 2:5-6 (KJV), "Trust in the Lord with all your heart; and lean not unto thine own understanding. In all thy ways acknowledge him, and he shall direct your paths."

The Desert
Shall Bloom

The desert shall blossom, and it is all because you are there. The people shall be glad for us (sons of God). Wherever the sons of God walk, they bring light and gladness of heart to the ones walking in the wilderness – those having wilderness experiences. As sons of God, when we come in contact with those that feel so alone, those walking in dry and dusty places, the life of Christ within us will make a change in their lives, and it is all because you are there. The life of God within you will bring about a change for the good, and it makes the people glad! For God is with you and in you, and His Spirit will be released from you to minister to any need they have. God will release His Spirit - just like a flower releasing its fragrance. The people will be blessed by the fragrance of the bloom (Holy Spirit). The desert shall blossom and bloom as a rose and it is all because you are there. "The wilderness and the solitary place shall be glad for them; and the desert shall rejoice, and blossom as the rose" (Isaiah 35:1 KJV).

The Growth of God's Seed

G od knows the intentions of your heart
And He knows when you're against a hurdle
But be not dismayed or be discouraged
For the "Seed" in you is fertile

God knows the paths and the way that you take
He knows every little heartache
But in spite of it, this "Seed" shall grow tall
An unbreakable promise to all

No borders or gates shall contain this "Seed"
And it shall grow green and spread as a vine,
Growing over fences and over the walls
Producing more seeds after its own kind

The "Seed" of the Lord shall cover the earth
And He shall send rain where He plants it
And an increase shall come to many nations
For God has declared and shall grant it!

The Incorruptible Seed

Jesus said, *"The seed is the word of God"* (Luke 8:11 KJV). The seed is "incorruptible," which means this seed is living, and will abide forever. It is not a "natural" seed that a farmer sows into the ground and decays, but it is a "spiritual" seed. This seed is eternal and will never decay (or become corruptible). This seed is imperishable (indestructible).

I've mentioned above several words to describe this seed: Incorruptible, imperishable, indestructible, eternal, life-giving, and immortal. Most of all, it is a "spiritual" seed, for it is the life of God!

It is through the living and abiding word of God that we are born again. Peter says that we are "being born again, not of corruptible seed, but of incorruptible, by the Word of God, which liveth and abideth forever" (1 Peter 1:23 KJV). To be "born again" means that a rebirth has taken place in your heart. It is a "spiritual" birth that happens in the heart by the power of the living God. The seed is Jesus Christ, the imperishable seed, who lives in our hearts.

The *incorruptible* word (seed) abides and lives forever, contrary to the natural corruptible seed that always decays and dies. Peter said "You have been regenerated (born again), not from a mortal origin (seed, sperm), but from one that is immortal by the ever living and lasting Word of God (1 Peter 1:23 AMP).

By the will of God, we are "quickened" - made alive by the incorruptible seed (the Holy Spirit). To quicken something is to bring it to life. Jesus said, "It is the spirit that quickeneth; the flesh profiteth nothing: the words that I speak unto you, they are spirit and they are life" (John 6:63 KJV). The incorruptible seed (itself) is always "life-giving." It is always active. "The word of God is quick, and powerful, and sharper than any two-edged sword, piercing even to the dividing asunder of soul and spirit, and of the joints and marrow, and is a discerner of the thoughts and intents of the heart" (Hebrews 4:12 KJV).

Just as a farmer sows a natural seed into the soil, the Word of God is sown in our hearts. It is usually a spoken word sown by an anointed minister of the gospel. He (or she) sows the seed of the Word in our hearts, then by the power of the Holy Spirit, the word comes alive. By faith when you receive Christ into your heart, you are "born again." Peter said, "The word of the Lord endureth forever, and this is the word which by the gospel is preached unto you" (1 Peter 1:25 KJV). God used the minister of the gospel to sow the seed.

"For this corruptible must put on incorruption, and this mortal must put on immortality. So when this corruptible shall have put on incorruption, and this mortal shall have put on immortality, then shall be brought to pass the saying that is written, Death is swallowed up in victory" (1 Corinthians 1:53-54 KJV). When this mortal puts on immortality, then death is destroyed, devoured, and consumed. We can say, "Victory in Jesus!"

The Light of Christ

The prophet, Ezekiel, spoke about the likeness of the living "beings" in 1:12-14 NIV). "Each one went straight ahead. Wherever the Spirit would go, they would go, without turning, as they went. The appearance of the living creatures (beings) was like burning coals of fire or like torches. Fire moved back and forth among them; it was bright, and lightning flashed out of it. The creatures (or beings) sped back and forth like flashes of lightning." What Ezekiel was speaking of was a body of believers walking in the Light of Christ, who moved, lived, and had their being IN HIM. They would be led straight ahead and not looking back. They would have the fire of the Holy Ghost and the power of God working within them. And in the realm of the Spirit, they would walk in obedience and by faith in God. An unlimited realm of the glory of God. No hindrances would stop them. And God would be sending them where they needed to be.

The Lord Is on Our Side

In a letter to Timothy from Paul, Paul said that the time would come that people would not endure sound teaching (Truth). They would turn their ears away (not listening for God's voice). They would wander off into myths and man-made fictions (not Truth). His friend (Demas) deserted him for the love of the world. Alexander (the coppersmith) did him wrong. At Paul's first trial, no one acted in his defense. All forsook him. But the Lord strengthened him & stood by him. If you feel forsaken and feel no one is for you, just stay calm and wait on the Lord, because if God is for you, who can be against you. The Lord is on your side and HE will strengthen you just as HE did Paul! That is the gospel of good news!

The Power of Kindness

Never underestimate the power of kindness
Those that have **not** are always the blindest
To be kind and giving in our deeds
Is like spreading tiny little apple seeds

With the breath of our kindness,
A light in the lamp takes on a new brightness
For words that are fitly spoken and right
Will cause many to be drawn to its light

The fruit of our kindness encompassing a city
Shows people with largeness of heart
Fences torn down and doors again open
Welcoming all and not just a part

The heart of the kind is like a drawing card
Drawing people like a moth to a flame
And the dazzling light of the kindness of words
Is like flowers springing up after a rain

Like a cloud full of water that empties itself
Refreshing us with words that we say
The riches of kindness poured out in the blindness
Turns Nighttime into a Day

We'll reap the rewards with seeds we have sown
The fruit of our lips we shall see
For casting our kindness among the blindest
Will surely come back unto me

JANELL BRYANT LAUGHLIN

The Treasures of Snow

In the Book of Job in the Old Testament, Job was a righteous man who was really tested by God, and God asked him this question, "Hast thou entered into the treasures of the snow?" (Job 38:22 KJV).

God referred to the snow as a treasure – something of great value.

All snowflakes are different, yet when individual snowflakes come together, they form a beautiful blanket covering the earth. I see this as a corporate body of believers coming together in the unity of the Spirit, functioning as "one" in the Holy Spirit. David said, "Behold, how good and how pleasant it is for brethren to dwell together in unity" (Psalms 133:1 KJV).

The color of snow is white and beautiful which represents purity - a people pure in heart. "Blessed are the pure in heart, for they shall see God" (Matthew 5:8 KJV).

The snowflakes always fall gently (and quietly) as they descend from the heavenly realm into the early realm. When God speaks to our heart about a thing, it is the time to be reverent and quiet. There is a time to keep silent. "A time to rend, and a time to sew; a time to keep silence, and a time to speak" (Ecclesiastes 3:7 KJV). Sometimes things are better left unsaid, for the use of vain words only produce noise (no life in them).

Sometimes Jesus opened not his mouth, yet His silence was more powerful than any vain, idle word.

God shows great love and mercy by sending the snow to keep the soil warm. It serves as a comforting blanket to protect the little plants from the severity of the cold frost, so the little plants will not become frost-bitten. "Give thanks unto the Lord, for he is good: for his mercy endureth forever" (Psalms 107:1 KJV).

When snow is melted, a change takes place. The snow melts and is changed into water. God's transforming power can melt a heart, and bring about a change in a life in an instant. When God asked Job to consider the treasures of the snow, in Job 38:22, I believe He wanted him to consider how God can take a life and turn it around, restore it, and create something beautiful.

"Come now, and let us reason together, saith the LORD: though your sins be as scarlet, they shall be as white as snow; though they be red like crimson, they shall be as wool" (Isaiah 1:18 KJV).

The "Trying" of Your Faith

The apostle Peter said, "The "trying" of our faith is more precious than gold that perishes." It creates in us stability to stand when our faith is tried. Here is a question God asked Jeremiah: "If you have run with footmen and they have tired you out, then how can you compete with horses? If you fall down in a land of peace, how will you do in the thicket of the Jordan?" (Jeremiah 12:5 NAS).

The "trying" of your faith takes place in the realm of the Spirit.

The apostle Paul said, "For we wrestle not against flesh and blood, but against principalities, against powers, against the rulers of the darkness of this world, against spiritual wickedness in high places" (Ephesians 6:12 KJV).

Peter said, "Beloved, do not be surprised at the fiery ordeal among you, which comes upon you for your testing, as though some strange thing were happening to you; but to the degree that you share the sufferings of Christ, keep on rejoicing; so that at the revelation of His glory, you may rejoice with exultation" (1 Peter 4:12 NAS). We are sharing the sufferings of Christ, but we can still rejoice with exultation which means we can say "woohoo" or "praise the Lord."

Every time we go through a trial, we can look back and say these words the Lord spoke to me as a song one morning: "Why should I worry? Why should I fret? Why should I worry and get so upset; God has been faithful; He's never failed me yet!"

Peter said to rejoice that you participate in the sufferings of Christ, so that you may be overjoyed when his glory is revealed! In you! There is a joy that awaits you after every trial because we know we are participating in the sufferings of Christ and are so "joined" with him that we become as "one." We are "taking part" of his sufferings! You feel what he feels, and He feels what you feel. It is good to know that he feels our infirmities. And we know that each trial will not last forever!

Peter said, "That the trial of your faith, being much more precious than of gold that perisheth, though it be tried with fire, might be found unto praise and honour and glory at the appearing of Jesus Christ" (I Peter 1:7 KJV). The "trying" of your faith is a precious thing, for it is bringing about a change inside of you. God wants a people pure (in heart). He wants our hearts so refined until the only thing that is left within is a pure heart, the nature of Christ.

David prayed, "Create in me a clean heart, O God; and renew a right spirit within me" (Psalms 51:10 KJV).

When a Silversmith holds a piece of gold in the fire, it is being purified. A change takes place in the fire, and it begins to melt. The heating of the gold only destroys the dross, leaving the "pure" alloy. When our faith has been "tried," the only thing left inside is a pure heart - Christ in us (the hope of glory).

Sometimes God will put us in situations we do not enjoy. He may put us in a red-hot fiery trial. There may be a spiritual heaviness that we feel in our spirit. This is the Holy Ghost fire working in us to produce the life of Christ. Jesus promised us that we would be baptized in the Holy Ghost *and fire*. It is during these dark times of the soul that we meet the Lord, and are being changed from glory to glory.

The apostle Paul wrote a letter to the Ephesians and said, "Above all, taking the shield of faith, wherewith ye shall be able to quench all the fiery darts of the wicked" (Ephesians 6:16 KJV). Paul was saying that you will be able to quench or "put out" the fiery darts of the evil one, if you put on your shield of faith.

Put on the whole armor that you may be able to stand against the many wiles (or strategies) of the devil. This shield of faith can quench (or extinguish) every fiery dart that is thrown at you. When you begin to study about the promises of God, your thoughts are toward him, and your mind will begin to take on a change, just like putting on a shield that a soldier wears to protect himself in battle. Spiritually speaking, this shield is our Lord Jesus Christ, the living Word. We need to hide the Word of God in our hearts before the battle, so when anything that is thrown at you, or if ugly words are spoken to you, you will be able to quench or "put out" what is being thrown against you.

"Consider it pure joy, my brothers and sisters, whenever you face trials of many kinds, because you know that the testing of your faith produces perseverance" (James 1:2-3 NIV). James goes on to say that the "trying" of your faith works patience. Then he said to "let patience finish its work so that you may be mature and complete, not lacking anything." Perseverance means "not giving up" even when it is hard, but to hang in there until God has accomplished what He has started in you. Can we count it all joy?

What a marvelous transformation takes place within us. As the ugly worm is turned into a beautiful butterfly, so we are changed from glory to glory by the Spirit of the Lord. Yield yourselves to the potter and watch him form the clay.

JANELL BRYANT LAUGHLIN

The Wilderness Experience

"Behold, I will do a new thing; now it springs forth; do you not perceive and know it, and will you not give heed to it? I will make a way in a wilderness, and rivers in the desert" (Isaiah 43:19 AMP).

A wilderness is a dry place, a solitary place. It has no springs of water to cause it to thrive. It is an uncultivated place, a deserted place, and barren. Many times we may feel deserted, as if we are going through a wilderness. We think we cannot go on any longer, maybe to the point of giving up. But just hold on! God is going to make a way where there seems to be no way, for He is The Way! "And a highway shall be there, and a way, and it shall be called the Holy Way; the unclean shall not pass over it, but it shall be for the redeemed; the wayfaring men, yes, the simple ones and fools, shall not err in it and lose their way" (Isaiah 35:8 AMP).

"The wilderness and the solitary place shall be glad for them; and the desert shall rejoice, and blossom as the rose" (Isaiah 35:1 KJV). The desert shall blossom, and it is because you are there. The people shall be glad for us (sons of God). Wherever the sons of God walk, they bring light and gladness of heart to the ones walking in the wilderness – those having wilderness experiences. As sons of God, when we come in contact with those that feel so alone, those walking in dry and dusty places, the life of Christ within us will make a change in their lives, and it is all because you are there. The life of God within you will bring about a change for the good, and it makes the people glad! For God is with you and in you, and His Spirit will be released from you to minister to any need they have. God will release His Spirit – just like a flower releasing its fragrance. The people will be blessed by the fragrance of the bloom (Holy Spirit). The desert shall blossom and bloom as a rose and it is all because you are there.

The bible says that one of our names shall be called: "Sought Out." You will be there for many who desperately need to hear a word "fitly" spoken. You will be there for many dry and thirsty people, and they will again be glad. "And they shall call them, *The Holy people, the redeemed of the Lord*; and thou shalt be called, *Sought Out, A city not forsaken*" (Isaiah 62:12 KJV).

David said, "The righteous shall flourish like the palm tree: he shall grow like a cedar in Lebanon" (Psalms 92:12 KJV). A palm tree will usually grow and flourish because of their massive root system, surviving hurricane-force winds. Cedar trees usually flourish and stay green all year-round because of water nearby. When you see cedar trees, there is usually water around some place. God will do miracles for you if you continually abide in Him and not be distracted by the world. If you abide (continually) in Him, the Lord said He would even plant a cedar in the wilderness for you. In your dry place, He will intervene on your behalf and give you strength to survive (even during your wilderness experience).

"Strengthen ye the weak hands, and confirm the feeble knees" (Isaiah 35:3 KJV). As a strong people in the Lord, we are to encourage others. When they become fearful, even to the point of trembling, our encouragement will help them stay on course and remain steady. One time during a battle with the Amalekites, Moses' hands grew heavy as he was holding up the rod to encourage the soldiers. His brother and high priest (Aaron) and Hur (Moses' companion) held his hands up (one on each side), so that his hands would remain steady. As long as Moses held his hands up, the Israelites were winning.

Isaiah prophesied, "I will open rivers in high places, and fountains in the midst of the valleys: I will make the wilderness a pool of water, and the dry land springs of water. I will plant in the wilderness the cedar…"(Isaiah 41:18-19 KJV). A river forms from water coming from a higher altitude. When the rain falls, it flows downhill, creating the river. Then the river flows "out" to the ocean. The river is always fresh because it is always flowing "out." Our Most High God wants us to abide in Him on a daily basis, and communicate with Him, because He loves us just as we love our children. We are in Him, and He is in us (as one). The river of life will flow "out" of us when we are abiding in Him (Christ Jesus). *"There's a river of life flowing out from me,"* as a song says.

Jesus said to the Samaritan woman at the well, "Everyone who drinks this water will be thirsty again, but whoever drinks the water I give them will never thirst. Indeed, the water I give them will become *in them* a spring of water welling up to eternal life" (John 4:13-14 NIV). The water that Jesus will give you will be *in you* a fountain springing up into everlasting life.

"For as the earth brings forth its bud, and as the garden causes the things that are sown in it to spring forth, so the Lord will cause righteousness and praise to spring forth before all the nations" (Isaiah 61:11 NKJV).

To Obey Is Better Than A Sacrifice

Abraham (a prophet) was chosen of God to become the father of a *spiritual* race. He was severely tested by God. He would have to make a hard decision to obey the Lord. God told him, "Take now your son, your only son, whom you love, Isaac, and go to the land of Moriah; and offer him there as a burnt offering on one of the mountains of which I will tell you" (Genesis 22:2 NAS).

Abraham obeyed the Lord commanded and saddled his donkey, and took two of his young men with him, and Isaac (his son); and he split wood for the burnt offering, and began his journey to take Isaac up to Mount Moriah, a high place which is referred to as a "land of vision" or a "hill."

On the third day of the journey, Abraham lifted up his eyes and saw the place from a distance. He told his servants to stay with the donkey while he and Isaac went up together to "worship," and he told them that they would be back again. Take notice here the words that Abraham spoke that was <u>full of faith</u>, "that they would be back again!"

Abraham took the wood for the burnt offering, and laid it on the shoulders of Isaac his son; and he took the fire (the firepot) in his hand and a knife, and the two of them walked on together, continuing their journey to the high place where Isaac was to be offered.

"And Isaac spake unto Abraham his father, and said, My father: and he said, Here am I, my son. And he said, Behold the fire and the wood: but where is the lamb for a burnt offering?" (Genesis 22:7 KJV). Abraham answered him and said, "My son, God will provide himself a lamb for a burnt offering: so they went both of them together" (Genesis 22:8 KJV). The two of them went on together, to the high place - the land of Moriah.

I can just imagine Isaac's thoughts at this point - trusting his father, never questioning his actions. I'm sure he was looking around for the lamb. But with a childlike faith, he trusted his father to tell the truth - that God would provide a sacrifice.

They arrived at the place God had told them to go – Mount Moriah. And there Abraham built an altar. He laid the wood (in order) and bound Isaac, his son, and laid him on the wood. He took the knife in his hand to slay Isaac.

This is the time he was severely tested. Abraham knew that God would provide Himself a lamb – even if He had to raise Isaac back up again. But trusting God and full of faith, he took the knife in his hand to slay Isaac, his only son, and an angel of the Lord called unto him from heaven and said, "Abraham, Abraham, Do not lay your hand on the lad, or do anything to him; for now I know that you fear and revere God, since you have not held back from ME or begrudged giving Me your son, your only son" (Genesis 22:12 AMP).

Abraham looked up and glanced around, and lo, behind him was a ram caught (or entangled) in a thicket by his horns. And Abraham went and took the ram, and offered it up for a burnt offering (instead of his son). God spared Isaac's life by providing a ram instead. God had provided a sacrifice. Abraham called the name of that place Jehovah-Jireh, which means *"The Lord will provide;"* and it is said to this day, "On the mount of the Lord it shall be provided." Abraham had intentions of slaying his only son and believed that God would have raised him from the dead. That's faith! He took God at his word and believed him. He walked in obedience to God's commands, and in doing this, it was accounted unto him for righteousness.

"By faith Abraham, when God tested him, offered Isaac as a sacrifice. He who had received the promises was about to sacrifice his one and only son, even though God had said to him, "It is through Isaac that your offspring will be reckoned." Abraham reckoned that God could raise the dead, and figuratively speaking, he did receive Isaac back from death" (Hebrews 11:17-19 NIV).

Figuratively speaking, Abraham did receive Isaac back from death (although the act of slaying was never carried out), for God intervened and provided a ram. But although God did not require Abraham to carry out the literal act of slaying Isaac, he did slay Isaac in his heart, for he had all intentions of proceeding with the knife. And because Abraham had intentions of doing the deed "in his heart," the deed was as good as a done. It was a done deal (figuratively speaking). Abraham obeyed and trusted God. He fulfilled what God had asked him to do. In his heart he obeyed God and was willing to do what God asked him to do. God tested his faith and Abraham remained true to God. He was faithful to God.

God in his mercy, has no delight in burn't sacrifices. He wants us to be a"living"_sacrifice, holy and true to Him, giving our lives on a daily basis dedicated to Him.

Samuel said, "Has the Lord as great a delight in burnt offerings and sacrifices, as in obeying the voice of the Lord? Behold, *to obey is better than sacrifice*, and to hearken is better than the fat of rams" (1 Samuel 15:22 AMP).

And an angel of the Lord called unto Abraham out of heaven a second time and said, "By Myself have I sworn, saith the Lord, for because you have done this thing, and have not withheld your only son, that in blessing, I will bless thee, and in multiplying I will multiply thy seed as the stars of the heaven, and as the sand which is upon the sea shore; and thy seed shall possess the gate of his enemies. And in thy Seed shall all the nations of the earth be blessed; because thou hast obeyed my voice" (Genesis 22:16-18 KJV). God could not have sworn by anyone greater than Himself. If you lay it all at the altar, you can come under the abundant blessings (or promises) he has provided. If you will be obedient to him, God will make provision for anything you need.

Abraham is called the "Father of Faith," because of obedience to the Lord. He obeyed the call!

"Now to Abraham and his Seed were the promises made. He saith not: "And to Seeds, as of many; but as of one, And to thy Seed, which is Christ" (Galatians 3:16 KJV). The Seed is Christ!

Two Men in The Earth

The apostle Paul said, "if there is a *natural* body, there is also a *spiritual* body." That is the two men in the earth - the natural man and the spiritual man. One is earthly; the other heavenly! One bears the image of the *earthly*; the other bears the image of the *heavenly*.

"And so it is written, The <u>first</u> man Adam was made a living soul; the <u>last</u> Adam was made a quickening spirit;

Howbeit, that was not first which is <u>spiritual</u>, but that which is <u>natural</u>; and afterward that which is spiritual;

The <u>first</u> man is of the earth, earthy; the <u>second</u> man is the Lord from heaven;

As is the <u>earthy</u>, such are they also that are earthy: and as is the <u>heavenly</u>, such are they also that are heavenly;

And as we have borne the image of the earthy, we shall also bear the image of the heavenly" (1 Corinthians 15:45-49 KJV).

Anything *earthy* (earthly) represents a low place. Anything *heavenly* represents a high place as the abode of God. I do not want to live in the basement of a house, but would rather live in the upstairs of the house. It is the same way in the Kingdom of God. If we abide "in Christ," we are living in a much higher level than the ones living in the basement of the house.

Life and peace IS an effect of being spiritually-minded, and having a clear conscience before God.

I heard about a farmer that was raising baby chickens and an eagle. He noticed that the chickens were always "looking down," pecking in the dirt on the ground (earthly) or (fleshly). The chickens represent a people who are bearing the image/likeness of the "earthly." On the contrary, eagles don't fit in with chickens, for they are born to bear the image/likeness of the heavenly realm. If God has called you to a higher walk, you are like that eagle, for an eagle instinctively knows that they were not born for the barnyard (a lower form of existence). As the eagle begins to grow, he feels a stirring (or a longing) for a higher place, for he is not content living on the earthly plane. He begins to "look up," and as the wind begins to blow, he lifts his wings and begins to soar up higher in heavenly places. In the wind (which represents the Spirit), he does not have to flap his wings or struggle. He just raises his wings, and the Lord does the rest. The wind carries him "in" it, just as we are carried "in Christ." From glory to glory the Lord is bringing about a change inside of us. That is the secret – being "in Christ." He gives us His strength and power to rise above any circumstance, as we have our minds firmly "fixed" on the prize of the high calling of God "in" Christ Jesus.

The Spiritual man focuses his attention on holy desires and purposes. The carnal-minded man (earthly-minded) man focuses his attention on things pertaining to the flesh. He is a natural-minded man with a love of sensual pleasures, always gratifying the flesh. He is walking in the image/likeness of the earthly, and yields to the nature of the flesh – gratifying itself. Anything it wants, it gets! When the apostle Paul was speaking to some weak believers, he said he could not talk to them as "spiritual" men, but had to talk to them as "babies in Christ," (unspiritual men). He had to feed them with "milk," and not with "meat," for they were not able to digest the meat of the Word. Then he told them that they were living like the world as unspiritual men, for where there was envying, strife, and divisions, they were carnal-minded. (From 1 Corinthians 1-3).

God's purpose for us was to be released from the enslaving power of our first birth (caused by the first Adam), in order to come under the authority of Christ (the last Adam), which is a heavenly, and peaceful state of mind.

One cannot please God if he is in the flesh (carnal-minded), with fleshly sensual appetites. "For to be carnally-minded is death; to be spiritually-minded is life and peace" (Romans 8:6 KJV).

"For since by man came death (through Adam); By man also came the resurrection of the dead (through Jesus); for as in Adam all die; even so in Christ shall all be made alive, but every man in his own order: Christ the first-fruits; afterward they that are Christ's at his coming" (1 Corinthians 15:21-23 KJV).

The apostle Paul was writing to those "In Christ," when he said, "Who hath delivered us from the power of darkness, and hath translated us into the kingdom of his dear Son, in whom we have redemption through His blood, even the forgiveness of sins" (Colossians 1:13-14 KJV). On the cross, God transferred (got it off of me) all sins and put it on Jesus' shoulders. By believing in Jesus, we have been "rescued" from the power of darkness and have been transferred into the kingdom of his beloved Son. "For God so loved the world, that he gave his only begotten Son, that whosoever believeth in him should not perish (die or be lost), but have everlasting life" (John 3:16).

"Therefore if any man be *in Christ*, he is a new creature: old things are passed away; behold, all things are become new" (2 Corinthians 5:17 KJV).

Walls of Jericho

What would you do if you looked up and saw a man standing in front of you with a drawn sword in his hand, and the man told you he was sent as a commander of the Army of the Lord, and had a message for you? I believe you would have a reverence for the Lord (a reverent fear of the Lord). I believe it would bring humility into your life immediately. You would probably do as Joshua did - fall on his face and worship the Lord. This is what happened to Joshua when he was near the city of Jericho. "Now, when Joshua was near Jericho, he looked up and saw a man standing in front of him with a drawn sword in his hand. Joshua went up to him and asked, 'Are you for us, or for our enemies?' "Neither," he replied, "but as commander of the army of the Lord I have now come." Then Joshua fell face down to the ground with a reverent fear of the Lord and asked him, "What message does my Lord have for his servant?" The commander of the Lord's army replied, "Take off your sandals, for the place where you are standing is holy." And Joshua did so! (Joshua 5:13-15 NIV).

The Lord said to Joshua, "See, I have given unto thine hand Jericho, and the king thereof, and the mighty men of valour" (Joshua 6:2 KJV). Jericho was a fenced-in city with high walls. The king of Jericho basically put the whole city on lock-down. None came in and none came out. All the gates were shut up tightly. As the children of Israel prepared to "go up against" the city of Jericho, God came to Joshua with a plan. The first thing the Lord told Joshua to do was to go around the city (with all the armed men) one time a day for six (6) days. In front of the Ark of the Covenant, seven priests carried seven trumpets of rams' horns, and they marched around the city for six days!

On the 7th day, the Lord told Joshua to go around the city as they did for the previous six days, but this day was going to be different on the seventh day. On the seventh day, they would march around the city not just one time, but <u>seven times</u>, with the priests blowing the trumpets (rams' horns). When they heard the priests sound a long blast on the trumpets, all the people were to give a loud shout. When all the people gave a loud shout, the wall of the city would crumble, and the Israelites would go straight in. After seven times marching around the city, the seven priests carrying the seven trumpets went marching forward. As they marched, they were blowing on their trumpets as the Lord commanded. The armed guard marched ahead of the priests who blew the trumpets, and the rear guard followed the Ark of the Covenant. The trumpets were sounding! But they were not to raise their voices (or shout) until he gave the command!

In obedience to the Lord, and as a man of great faith, Joshua gave the signal for the people to "Shout; for the Lord hath given you the city" (Joshua 6:16 KJV). The people gave a shout, with the priests blasting on their trumpets. After hearing the sound of the trumpets, and the people shouting with a great shout, the walls of Jericho fell flat. The wall collapsed, so every man charged straight in, and they took the city. They devoted the city to the Lord, and destroyed with the sword every living thing in it – men and women, young and old, cattle, sheep and donkeys. They destroyed every living thing in the city, except Rahab (a woman known as a harlot). Her life was spared because she had hidden the two spies that Joshua had sent as spies to Jericho. She was spared, and all of her family.

The wall will always yield to God. It was *by faith* (not by force) the walls of Jericho came down.

The Lord spoke these words to me one morning as I was praying for a young lady that needed some walls to come down in her life. He said to tell her, "When you feel as if you can't go on any longer about a situation, that's when God's grace kicks in and carries you the rest of the way." God's grace was sufficient!

When you get to that place when you feel like God has brought you to a "nothingness," and you want God to intervene for you, but you realize that it cannot be done in your own strength, then God will show His strength. He will cause the walls to come down just for you because you have been faithful. Whatever the problem is will crumble! Even if you have to go around it one more time, or seven more times. Hold on, for He will cause you to be victorious, even if he has to remove the obstacle in your way. At the appointed time when God signals, the walls are coming down, for God will finish (complete) what he has started in you. Wait for it for it will surely come! As the Lord said to Joshua, "I have given unto thine hand Jericho," he will give it unto you.

Washing of Regeneration

The apostle Paul talks about a washing of water (by the Word). "That he might sanctify and cleanse it with the washing of water by the word" (Ephesians 5:26 KJV). It is a continual washing with water (through the Word of God). This washing takes place from the inside out by the Holy Spirit of God. God wants to wash us clean!

This "washing of regeneration" is a "spiritual" washing that is taking place inside. It is the very life of God that is imparted into us. We are His workmanship, and His work begins in the heart -from inside out. When a person believes in the Lord Jesus Christ, he is born anew. He is born again! God begins to change his old nature into a new nature. That's what "Regeneration" means: A new birth; a renewal; a restoration. He takes what he already has, and makes it anew. "A new heart also will I give you, and a new spirit will I put within you: and I will take away the stony heart out of your flesh, and I will give you an heart of flesh, and I will put my spirit within you, and cause you to walk in my statutes, and ye shall keep my judgments, and do them" (Ezekiel 36:26-27 KJV). God will *renew* that hard, cold, and rebellious heart into a soft, warm and tender one. God can *restore* that stony heart and make it into a new vessel that He can use for His glory.

When I am born "again," I'm a new creation, a brand new man. Old things have passed away and I've been born again. It's like I have been awakened from a deep sleep. Once I was blind, but now I see! There has been an *enlightening* by the Holy Spirit, and I begin to understand spiritual matters. It is a spiritual awakening. Once I felt far away from God, but now I have an awareness that he is nigh at hand. I felt alienated (cut off) from the life of the quickening power of Christ Jesus, but now he is no longer estranged (a stranger) to me, and he is my friend. I have a boldness to come before him, and approach him anytime.

At regeneration, man receives God's own life into his spirit and is born of God. He is "born again." A new birth has taken place in his spirit.

In 1 Peter 1:23 (KJV) he said, "Being born again, not of corruptible seed, but of incorruptible, by the word of God, which liveth and abideth forever." You have been regenerated (born again), not by the seed of the "natural" man, but by the seed of the Holy Ghost, the "spiritual" seed, the seed that is imperishable and lives forever.

The Washing of Regeneration is a "spiritual" baptism – a baptism into Christ!

I have heard someone say that if you catch a pig, bring him in, wash him and clean him on the outside, he will look good. But if you let him go back outside, he will return to the same old mud. He loves wallowing in the mud! Does that sound like someone you know? He was not changed from within but only on the outside. Some people are like the dirty pig because they haven't been changed on the inside. We cannot change ourselves, sad to say, but God will do the changing if we yield ourselves to the Holy Spirit, pray and seek his face for the change to come. The Light of Christ will begin to bring about a change by His Spirit. Have you ever wondered how a beautiful butterfly can be transformed from an ugly caterpillar? God is greater than any stronghold in your life.

By the washing of regeneration (by His holy Spirit), we are now partakers of this generation with God's genes in us praise God. "But ye are a chosen generation, a royal priesthood, an holy nation, a peculiar people; that ye should shew forth the praises of him who hath called you out of darkness into his marvelous light: which in time past were not a people, but are now the people of God: which had not obtained mercy, but now have obtained mercy" (1 Peter 2:9-10 KJV).

A "washing of regeneration" is a spiritual washing by the Holy Spirit. A new birth has taken place inside. He has been "born again." Jesus said, "Verily, verily, I say unto thee, Except a man be born again, he cannot see the kingdom of God." Jesus also said, "Except a man be born of water and of the Spirit, he cannot enter into the kingdom of God. That which is born of the flesh is flesh; and that which is born of the Spirit is spirit. Marvel not that I said unto thee, Ye must be born again" (John 3:5-7 KJV). Jesus was saying here that there is a "natural" birth, but there is also a "spiritual" birth that takes place within that transforms a person and washes him clean.

Mankind was once de-generated into a fleshly position, because of the fall of Adam, and we needed a Savior to bring us back from a fallen state. He had to be a Savior without sin, a Savior without a spot, wrinkle or blemish. Jesus Christ was the one we needed for He was without sin, and I thank him for the shedding of his blood. Only HE could bring about a "washing of re-generation."

In Paul's letter to Titus, he wrote that when the kindness and love of God our Saviour appeared, he saved us in his mercy, "Not by works of righteousness which we have done, but according to his mercy he saved us, by the washing of regeneration, and renewing of the Holy Ghost, which he shed on us abundantly through Jesus Christ our Saviour" (Titus 3:5-6) KJV. He saved us in his mercy - not by any achievement of our own, not by our good works.

The old man – the former nature (a degenerate, unrenewed self).

The new man - the new nature (a regenerate, renewed self).

Paul said to "Be renewed in the spirit of the mind; and that you put on the new man which after God is created in righteousness and true holiness" (Ephesians 4:23-24 KJV). The old man is corrupt by its deceitful desires, but God can change all that. When we put on the new man, a rebirth takes place inside of us by the power of the Holy Ghost, bringing about a change in our attitudes, our thinking. He gets rid of our stinkin' thinkin'.

"Therefore if any man be in Christ, he is a new creature: old things are passed away; behold, all things are become new" (2 Corinthians 5:17 KJV). In Christ, a man's heart is made new. From the moment the re-birth takes place in our hearts (by the Spirit), all things begin to take on a change. The old is left behind! His heart is like a house that has been renovated (regenerated). God is the potter; I am the clay. He molds me and makes me into His very own image and what he sees is Christ. The NIV says, "Therefore, if anyone is in Christ, he is a new creation; the old has gone, the new has come."

That which is born of the flesh is flesh! That which is born of the Spirit is Spirit!

Lightning Source UK Ltd.
Milton Keynes UK
UKHW042128310822
408116UK00010B/179